# A
# REASONABLE
# FAITH

# BOOKS OF INTEREST BY N.E. KURZ

## Stand in the Gap Trilogy

Book 1 - *A Parallel Time & Place*: *A Story of a
Modern Nation Running in Sync with a Biblical
Land in an Alternate Reality* (2025)
ISBN: 979-8-9905216-0-5 HC; 979-8-995216-1-2 PB;
979-8-9905216-2-9 Ebook - Kindle

Book 2 - *The Ezekiel Factor*: *Judgement Precedes Grace*
(Forthcoming, Fall 2027) ISBN: 979-8-9905216-3-6 HC

## Window of Opportunity Trilogy

Book 1 - *A Personal Grief*: *Finding Faith Through Loss* (2025)
ISBN: 979-8-9905216-4-3 PB;
ISBN: 979-8-9905216-7-4 Ebook - Kindle

Book 3 - *A Perilous Time*: *Keeping Faith During
Periods of Adversity* (Forthcoming, Summer 2025)
ISBN: 979-8-9905216-5-0 PB;
ISBN: 979-8-9905216-8-1 Ebook - Kindle

Window of Opportunity Trilogy

Book 2

# A
# REASONABLE
# FAITH

Finding Faith Through Rational Evidence

N. E. KURZ

**DOGWOOD PUBLISHING**
BOLIVAR, MISSOURI 65613

Published by Dogwood Publishing, Bolivar, MO 65613

"Scripture taken from the NEW AMERICAN STANDARD BIBLE, © 1960, 1962, 1963, 1968, 1971, 1972, 1973, 1975, 1977 by The Lockman Foundation. Used by permission."
www.Lockman.org

Printed in the United States of America.

Library of Congress Control Number: 2024938908

Publisher's Cataloging-in-Publication data

Names: Sawyers-Kurz, Norma Eileen, author.
Title: A Reasonable Faith : Finding Belief Through Rational Evidence / Norma Eileen Sawyers-Kurz.
Series: Window of Opportunity Trilogy
Description: Bolivar, MO: Dogwood Publishing, 2025.
Identifiers: LCCN: 2024938908 | ISBN: 979-8-9905216-6-7 (paperback) | 979-8-9905216-9-8 (Kindle)
Subjects: LCSH Faith. | Christian life. | Apologetics. | BISAC RELIGION / Christian Living / General | RELIGION / Christian Theology / Apologetics Classification: LCC BV4905.3 .S29 2025 | DDC 248.8/6--dc23

# DEDICATION

To my husband John, who
not only supports me in my writing,
but also gives me lovely flowers.

# CONTENTS

| | | |
|---|---|---|
| 1 | Why Do We Need To Reason Our Faith? | 1 |
| 2 | Is it Wrong to Doubt or to Question? | 23 |
| 3 | Is It Enough to Just Believe? | 31 |
| 4 | Is Christianity Just a Psychological Crutch? | 41 |
| 5 | Are All Religions True? | 49 |
| 6 | Does the Bible Conflict With Science? | 57 |
| 7 | Was Jesus Really God? | 67 |
| 8 | Why Does God Allow Evil & Suffering? | 77 |
| 9 | Is the Bible Truly God's Word? | 87 |
| 10 | What Is God Like? | 97 |
| 11 | Why Do Some Professed Believers Fall Astray? | 107 |
| Notes | | 111 |

# 1

# WHY DO WE NEED TO REASON OUR FAITH?

There are several important reasons why individuals may need to think through or reason their beliefs. Although some people become Christians simply by believing on authority, in our modern age there are others who truly need to ask and to receive in-depth answers to questions about God before making a decision in regard to their faith.

Importantly, scripture agrees that we should think through our faith, by pointing out that Christians are to "always be prepared to give an answer to everyone who asks you to give the reason for the hope that you have. But do this with gentleness and respect."[1] So, the first reason we are to think through our faith is because the bible tells Christians to be prepared to share the basics of our faith with others, but to do so in love, not in harshness or disrespect.

An example of the need to search for truth is displayed in the story of my own personal experience. In *A Personal Grief: Finding Faith Through Loss*, the first book of my "Window of Opportunity Trilogy," I share what occurred in my life that propelled me to search for answers about God. After my daughter Karen's untimely death, which resulted from injuries received in a tragic motorcycle/truck accident, I struggled to find answers to questions I had (some from as early as my childhood) about Ultimate Reality. Here is an excerpt:

> It continued to be difficult for me to function at every day tasks while searching for seemingly unobtainable answers about life: *Why did this tragedy happen to my daughter? How did God fit into the picture? Was there really a God who cared?* Anxiety over profound questions of this type tore at my soul night and day.
>
> Few moments of consciousness existed for me that my mind was not churning these uncertainties over and over. But where could I find help? Finally, the realization dawned on me that perhaps I could pray to God for help with this problem. If God was truly accessible, maybe He would help me find answers. Three months after Karen's death, I got up from bed one night at 3:00 a.m. to ask for help in understanding. In desperation I prayed that God, if he was really "there," would help me in my search for spiritual truth.
>
> A most remarkable thing happened the afternoon after my prayer for spiritual assistance. Previously I wrote about Karen and me reading together the *Reader's Digest* version of *Song for Sarah* by Paula D'Arcy. Soon after Karen's death, I bought the book version. I had noticed the preliminaries of *Song for Sarah* included an endorsement by a man named Sheldon Vanauken who was extolling the value of Mrs. D'Arcy's book.
>
> I mention this because of something which happened later the same day of my prayer for spiritual guidance. Deciding to go shopping at the large mall of a nearby city,

I found my curiosity aroused when I "accidentally" noticed the book, *A Severe Mercy*, by Sheldon Vanauken, the man just mentioned. Under the name of the book and the author were these words: "Includes eighteen previously unpublished letters by C. S. Lewis." Although I'd never heard of C. S. Lewis, I assumed he must be someone very famous and important. Later, spying a book by this author, I impulsively decided to purchase both books.

Back at home reading the two books that night, I was totally amazed. Vanauken explained in his book how he and his wife went through a search for spiritual truth and answers. Corresponding with C. S. Lewis, Vanauken asked many philosophical questions about Christianity, and Lewis answered the questions by letter. It was remarkable that Vanauken asked him some of the same questions that had troubled me.

For example, in *A Severe Mercy*, Vanauken asked C. S. Lewis the question of whether Christianity is the only true religion. . . . As I read Lewis' clear answers to this and other questions, and as I later read his numerous books, everything started making sense to me. Lewis was the first Christian I had ever encountered who shared how he had "thought through" or" reasoned" his beliefs. Reading his books, I could see real answers did exist to my problem questions about Christianity.[2]

Miraculously, the Lord had helped me in my search for truth by directing me to the writings of C. S. Lewis, the great Christian apologist and writer.

A contemporary author making a long search for truth is Deborah Cusick, author of *Beyond the Ends of the Earth*. To gain firsthand knowledge of other religions and to determine which worldview was correct, she visited 39 nations.

Growing up in a traditional church, she said that "the concept I developed of God when I was young wasn't very favorable. I never saw Him as loving or compassionate and wanting to be known. I didn't trust that He was good. I thought he was angry and vengeful. In my religious upbringing, we were taught that God was too complex to be understood. Our church leaders needed to interpret Him for us, but I never quite understood the interpretation."[3] She also laments: "How I wish I had had someone to guide me, to share what they'd learned along the road of life."[4]

And, I think that's why she and I have written our respective books: We both hope that others can learn from our experiences. In my own case, since I understand first-hand the current deemphasis on religious questioning, I've written this book on the Christian concepts of "faith" and "reason."

During my painful struggle for spiritual answers, I became aware that the relationship of faith (belief) to reason (knowledge) is widely misunderstood by great numbers of contemporary Christians who seem to feel that knowledge is not as important as believing, or having faith. Viewing evangelism as mostly an emotional process, rather than a process necessitating intelligent knowledge both of God and of the world, they have forgotten the function of reason in conversion; and, also, in daily Christian living and loving.

The great Christian doctrines are not just claims of important moral teaching; they are facts which are inseparably linked to actual events of the past. If Christianity is true, it is because the Christian faith is founded on fact—real historical happenings as reported by the apostles. Chief among these is the resurrection of Jesus, the supreme fact of all history. Because Christianity claims to be objectively true, factual knowledge and historical evidence are important elements to distinguish the truth claims of Christianity from other religions. In a pluralistic world, an objective approach to the spreading of the Gospel is desperately needed, one that will give the non-Christian clear ground for trying Christianity.

In *Faith Founded on Fact*, John Warwick Montgomery asks "what is the non-Christian to do, when amid this din he hears the Christian message: Are we Christians so naïve as to think that he will automatically, *ex opere operato*, accept Christianity as true and put away world-views contradicting it? And if we call out to him, 'Just try Christianity and you will find that it proves itself experientially,' do we really think that he will not at the same time hear precisely the same subjective-pragmatic appeal from numerous other quarters?"[5]

Separating faith from reason, Christians are left with "individual opinion" which is merely subjectively or personally verifiable, if that. Rendered defenseless to support their claims in relation to the great number of world religions also claiming to be subjectively verifiable, about all such Christians can do to "share" their faith is to say, "My religion is true for me." But adherents to opposing religions will also say, "Mine is true for me, so why should I accept your Christianity?"

And therefore, we turn to the second reason people need to think through or reason their beliefs. People who know little about Christianity, those living both here and abroad, need solid reasons for making a commitment to the Christian faith. Rather than expecting these men and women to accept the Christian message merely on the basis of our personal experience, believers should support important Christian claims to truth by the knowledgeable evidence of reason. Montgomery goes on to say:

> Absolute proof of the truth of Christ's claims is available only in personal relationship with Him, but contemporary man has every right to expect us to offer solid reasons for making a total commitment. The apologetic task is justified as a ground for faith, as a means by which the objective truth of God's Word can be made clear so that men will heed it as the vehicle of the Spirit who convicts the world through its message.[6]

Paul Little, in *Know Why You Believe*, also states that "our personal subjective experience is based on objective historical fact."[7] What matters is not how much subjective experience or personal faith we have, but how much rational evidence or objective truth we can share. Faith must be based on good reasons. After all, the Lord wants us to share our faith with others worldwide. That's why scripture says: "All the nations you have made will come and worship before you, Lord; they will bring glory to your name. For you are great and do marvelous deeds; you alone are God."[8]

The bible also states that "the Lord is the great God, the great king above all gods. In his hand are the depths of the earth, and the mountain peaks belong to him. The sea is his, for he made it, and his hands formed the dry land."[9] In other words, scripture is saying here that God is truly above all other (so-called) gods, for there is no corner of the Universe that is not in His hand. Yet, pagan people world-wide invented various gods for different people groups, different geographic regions, different cosmic areas, and different aspects of life such as war, fertility, and so forth.

But, believe it or not, the same holds true today. There are millions of modern people worldwide who still adhere to these pagan gods. Hence, the third reason God wants us to think through our beliefs is so that we can do a better job of sharing the evidence for our faith with the large numbers of mankind still clinging to false deities.

Recently, the world's largest religious gathering took place in India's northern city of Prayagraj at the Maha Kumbh festival. The event is held every 12 years at the confluence of the Ganges, Yamuna, and the mythical Saraswati rivers. Here is a report about the festival that appeared in *Newsweek*:

> Millions of Hindu devotees, mystics, and holy men and women have flocked to . . . Prayagraj to kickstart the [Maha Kumbh] religious gathering [of] at least 400 million—more than the population of the United States—according to officials.[10]

Amazingly, that is around 200 times the number of pilgrims that flooded the Muslim holy cities of Mecca and Medina in Saudi Arabia for the annual Hajj pilgrimage last year as reported in the news.

The Maha Kumbh festival has its roots in a Hindu tradition that says "the god Vishnu wrested a golden pitcher containing the nectar of immortality from demons. These drops are believed to have fallen in Prayagraj, Nasik, Ujjain, and Haridwar, the four rotating festival sites."[11] That's why every 12 years Hindu pilgrims gather at the confluence of the sacred rivers to "take a holy dip on the auspicious dates of the Maha Kumbh [because that] is believed to wash away sins and grant you Moksha"[12]

Hence, Bhagwat Prasad Tiwari, a festival pilgrim said "We feel peaceful here and attain salvation from the cycles of life and death."[13] Here,Tiwari was making a subjective claim, rather than an objective claim, that his religion was true.

However, pilgrims to Maha Kumbh also include large numbers of attendees from beyond the land of India, including "one visitor who made headlines, Apple heiress and philanthropist Laurene Powers Jobs, the widow of Steve Jobs, who [planned] to stay for a couple of weeks ... and take part in rituals, according to her guru Swami Kailashananda Giri, head of the Niranjani Akhara Monastery."[14] News accounts such as this help us realize the enormity of the task ahead for Christians, because truly, there are many adherents to other religions, from around the world, who need to hear truth.

However, the fourth reason we need to think through our faith involves the following verse: "My people are destroyed for lack of knowledge."[15] A lack of knowledge of God's Word can lead to apostasy, because when people are unsure of the reasons for their faith, they may either drift away from God, or on the other hand, be drawn into false religion. Thus, lack of knowledge of the truth can lead people astray from God.

Apostacy, in turn, gives God the right to bring charges against the inhabitants of nations such as ancient Judah or modern America that have been blessed by God but have nevertheless turned away from Him. That sentiment is based on the truth of the bible that where apostasy reigns, "there is no faithfulness, no love, no acknowledgement of God in the land. There is only cursing, lying, murder, stealing and adultery, they break all bounds, and bloodshed follows bloodshed. Because of this the land dries up, and all who live in it waste away."[16]

Scripture here continues to point out in a figurative way that judgment can fall on a nation blessed by God if that nation abandons Him and His moral precepts: "A whirlwind will sweep them [the wicked] away."[17] That is figurative language for an apostate country that may soon be destroyed by God as a nation, "like chaff swirling from a threshing floor."[18] For "the wicked are like chaff that the wind blows away,"[19] a simile of the wretchedness of the chaff being carried away by the lightest wind, and its removal bringing about cleansing by extracting what is utterly useless.

Thus, we become more fully aware of why American Christians so desperately need to personally share the foundations for their faith with others: The Lord, the Maker of the universe, has the right to refine America in a similar manner to the way He refined Judah when the people of that nation went into Babylonian exile.

Ancient Judah at that time had progressively become so depraved that the Lord knew it would soon reach the point of no return. In fact, the people of Judah and Jerusalem had reverted so far away from God that He had to raise up a reforming king to give the people another chance to return to Him. All of this was predicted in 1 Kings 13 when a man of God from Judah gave a prophetic announcement of the future rule of King Josiah, who came to the throne in Judah nearly 300 years later.

In Jeremiah 18:1-4, the prophet Jeremiah made an announcement from God in what could be termed a parable in action. This is the word that came to Jeremiah from the Lord: "'Go down to the potter's house, and there I will give you my message.' So I went down to the potter's house, and I saw him working at the wheel. But the pot he was shaping from the clay was marred in his hands; so the potter formed it into another pot, shaping it as seemed best to him."

As I read Jeremiah's description of the incident at the potter's house where a potter was using a wheel to form his clay into a pot, I recalled a pottery course I took in college. In Pottery 1, we students tried to be "lords" over our clay as we set about the task of learning how to use a pottery wheel. But since we hadn't yet learned how to position our hands and fingers steadily to form a clay jar, our clay was repeatedly "marred" in our hands.

Hence, we were forced to discard the forming of that particular jar. At that point, all we could do was to form a ball out of the marred clay, work with it to remove air bubbles, and then attempt to make a new jar. Over and over, we made effort after effort until finally we became more adept at forming clay vessels on a wheel.

Returning to Jeremiah's announcement from the Lord, he then explained that the word of the Lord came to him again:

> He said,"Can I not do with you, as this potter does?" declares the Lord. "Like clay in the hand of the potter, so are you in my hand. If at any time I announce that a nation or kingdom is to be uprooted, torn down, and destroyed, and if that nation I warned repents of its evil, then I will relent and not inflict on it the disaster I had planned. And if at another time I announce that a nation or kingdom is to be built up and planted, and if it does evil in my sight and does not obey me, then I will reconsider the good I had intended to do for it."[20]

Here scripture explains that world nations are like clay in a potter's hands. The promises or the threats of God toward nations are conditioned on human actions. God, who Himself does not change, nevertheless can change his response to people depending on what they do or don't do.

But scripture also tells us the Lord had compassion on the people of Jerusalem and Judah during that apostate period, for he gave them a window of opportunity to turn back to him and raised up Josiah, a young son of evil King Amon, to be a reforming king as scripture had foretold. The book of the law was discovered during Josiah's reign (see 2 Kings 22 and 2 Chronicles 34:14-31) and reforms occurred throughout Judah (See 2 Kings 23:1-25 and 2 Chronicles 34:1-13 and 35:1-19).

However, after King Josiah's death, the nation of Judah fell back into apostasy. Why? Because the hearts of many of the people hadn't been truly aligned with God. Outwardly they were conforming to Josiah's reforms, but inwardly they were still apostate in their hearts. So, after Josiah's death many of those in his household and administration reverted to their idolatrous ways again. Without King Josiah over them to direct them toward God, they returned to their evil ways.

Basically, many of the elite class and leadership went astray because they'd never turned to God in the first place. So, for some people the reform was outward, not inward. Yet, the reform movement of Josiah gave Jerusalem and Judah more time. God wanted the people to have more time so they could return to their Maker. Thus, even though some of the elite refused to return to God in their hearts, it is probable that more of the ordinary people reverently and sincerely made God the Lord of their lives at that time.

Anyway, after King Josiah's death, "the people of the land took Jehoahaz, son of Josiah, and anointed him and made him king in place of his father."²¹ He was an evil king, as were the kings following him, which included Jehoiakim, Jehoiachin, and Zedekiah, who was on the throne when Jerusalem and Judah fell (See 2 Kings 23:31-37 and 24:1-20).

Scripture states that "it was because of the Lord's anger that all this [Jerusalem and Judah's fall] happened."[22]

J. Andrew Dearman, author of *The NIV Application Commentary: Jeremiah and Lamentations*, notes that God's judgment of Judah can be instructive to modern nations as well as to ancient Judah:

> One of the stupendous events of the twentieth century happened with the collapse of Soviet domination of Eastern Europe, beginning with the fall of the Berlin Wall in November 1989. The impact of this collapse is still being worked out. Each state has its own version of the impact as do the churches in the region. . . . No Christian should doubt the role of God in this process; the contribution of churches to the collapse is widely recognized. Here is a paradigm of the surprising providence of God being worked out. Was the collapse predicted in the Old Testament? Not precisely, but the God who reshapes history and speaks authoritatively is revealed in the Old Testament and he is still at work.[23]

Therefore, in a similar manner to what occured in ancient Judah, by the providence and compassion of God, it seems spiritually declining America has been given an opportunity to postpone the Lord's pending judgment of the U. S. The American people have elected reforming president, Donald Trump, who along with his administration are feverishly working to reform our land. And the secular reforms they do will also provide a window for spiritual reforms in our land.

That's the fifth reason we should be ready to share our faith in a knowledgeable way. We need to truly understand the foundations upon which our faith rests. Then we can share our faith in such a way that it readies seekers of truth for a genuine inward conversion of their hearts, if they so choose.

An online article titled: "How President Donald Trump's brush with death turned his faith into fire," reports some of what is happening in our nation:

> It's holy week and President Donald Trump isn't just leading the country, he is leaning hard into the belief that he's been chosen to do so: 'I believe my life was saved that day in Butler for a good reason,' he declared during his address to a joint session of Congress last month. . . . It's a sentiment that's becoming central to Trump's second term. At the National Prayer Breakfast in February, Trump reflected more personally: 'It changed something in me, I feel. I feel even stronger. I believed in God, but I feel much more strongly about it.'[24]

President Trump "credits his upbringing as a Presbyterian for instilling his sense of morality, and as he tells it, his destiny. . . . He recalled attending Sunday School, watching Billy Graham crusades, and being raised by a devout Scottish mother and a 'very strong' but 'great-hearted' father."[25] Trump also noted:

> 'I was blessed to be raised in a churched home . . . and that faith lives on in my heart every single day,' Trump added. That foundation, he argues, is critical not just for him personally, but for the soul of the country. In an August 2024 sit-down with Fox News host Laura Ingraham, he said bluntly: 'One of the reasons that our country has lost, sort of everything, it's lost so much, is we don't have religion to the same extent.' Trump often returns to the government's role during the pandemic as a flashpoint. People weren't

even allowed to meet outside [for church]. They'd [the current liberal government] arrest everybody. . . . They were horrible,' he said. 'That was a very bad time for organized religion.'[26]

Trump has also used his presidency to advocate for religious liberty as a cornerstone of his leadership:

'As long as I'm president, no one is going to stop you from practicing your faith or from preaching what is in your heart,' he said in his first term in 2017. And he has echoed that promise ever since. 'Faith inspires us to be better, to be stronger, to be more caring and giving. . . . It is time to put a stop to the attacks on religion.' Trump made international religious freedom a consistent part of his agenda, too. In a 2017 interview with Christian Broadcasting Network CBN host David Brody, Trump focused on persecuted Christians. . . . 'We are going to help them.'[27]

And, Trump continues to link America's founding ideals directly to faith: "Our Declaration of Independence proclaims that our rights are bestowed on us by our Creator. Each time we pledge allegiance to our flag, we say that we are one nation under God."[28] At the National Prayer Breakfast in 2017, he added that "freedom is not a gift from the government, but that freedom is a gift from God. America will thrive as long as we continue to have faith in God."[29]

Comments such as that indicate Trump realizes the spiritual danger America faces. "Over the past two years, Trump has repeatedly sounded the alarm over America's spiritual decline."[30] Thus, we're provided with the sixth reason American Christians need to reason their faith: The Christians of the United States need to realize the spiritual danger America faces at the present time in history. Time may be short for us to share our faith freely.

Trump also understands that his relationship with God has become personal and God's plan for him is providential. Regarding the Butler assassination attempt on his life, "according to Trump it wasn't just a lucky turn of the head, it was divine intervention. As he tells it, he looked toward a chart at just the right moment. 'God did that. I mean, it had to be.'"[31]

Therefore, that online article noted in its headline that "President Trump's brush with death turned his faith into fire."[32] Of course, there are people who may doubt the authenticity of Trump's faith because they disagree with some things he says or disapprove of his manner. Also, Trump enjoys lightening up situations at times by joking, but some people apparently don't have a sense of humor.

Others don't seem to realize God chooses whom he wants to carry out His will. In the Old Testament when Daniel was captive in Babylon, he knew that although Babylonian King Nebuchadnezzar seemed to have power on a human plane over Judah, the truth was that Nebuchadnezzar became king because God is the One who "deposes kings and raises up others."[33]

Nevertheless, realizing how some feel about Trump, I prayed God would help me know if I should include the part about him in my book. At the end of the prayer, I also requested that the Lord would supply me with an appropriate hymn for the day. Following is the hymn, which I'd never heard before, to which I opened my hymnal:

"Set My Soul Afire"

Set my soul afire, Lord, for Thy Holy Word, burn it deep within me, let your voice be heard; Millions grope in darkness in this day and hour, I will be your witness, fill me with Thy Pow'r.

Set my soul afire, Lord, set my soul afire, make my life a witness of Thy saving pow'r. Millions grope in darkness, waiting for Thy Word, Set my soul afire, Lord, Set my soul afire.

Set my soul afire, Lord, for the lost in sin, give to me a passion as I seek to win; Help me not to falter, never let me fail, Fill me with Thy Spirit, let Thy will prevail.

Set my soul afire, Lord, set my soul afire, make my life a witness of Thy saving pow'r. Millions grope in darkness, waiting for Thy Word, Set my soul afire, Lord, Set my soul afire.[34]

Since I'd never heard the hymn before, I turned to my computer and googled "Set My Soul Afire." And then, as tears streamed down my face, I joined in singing along with a church choir as they sang this beautiful old hymn. Now I knew the Lord had answered my prayer.

Scripture tells us God's fire is meant to ignite His people with a passion for His purposes for mankind. Following Christ's resurrection, He informed His followers that He would send the Holy Spirit to empower people to effectively carry out his intention to spread the good news worldwide. On the day of Pentecost the Holy Spirit was sent to empower the people, and you can read about it in Acts 2.

One of the signs of the Spirit's arrival was what appeared to be tongues of fire that came to rest on each participant who was filled by the Holy Spirit. Although that particular sign of fire occurred only on that occasion, the spiritual empowerment that began at Pentecost continues through Spirit-filled followers of Christ to this day and fills Christians with the desire and ability to carry out Christ's commands to spread the gospel.

Therefore, I think it is by the mercy and compassion of the Lord that we have been given a window of opportunity to share our faith. Hopefully, after Trump's presidency, Americans will continue to vote for good leadership in America. However, we can't take that for granted, so if in the future far-left leadership does come back into power, there's danger that'll bring our nation back to the brink again.

This is because, as alluded to earlier, when our great nation was first formed, our founding fathers set up our government to run according to conservative principles, based on the tenets of God's moral law as set forth in scripture. The founders felt they'd come to America as to "a land of promise" for those who believe in Jesus Christ. And, they established a nation and a form of government that has given us the greatest nation in world history.

Yet, especially in the last twenty-five years, our great nation has drifted away from those principles. Our country has changed from a religious one, where almost everyone believed in God, into a more secularized society rife with woke issues such as diversity, gender, social justice, and free speech issues, along with others rooted in socialist and Marxist beliefs that deny God's righteous decrees. These things aren't just happening, they've been orchestrated to tear apart the moral and spiritual fabric of America.

Woke agendas, such as allowing unrestricted immigration and permitting boys to play in female sports are also endangering our people. Likewise, there are attempts to destroy the nuclear family, to promote racial conflict, to neuter the police, and to destabilize the existing social order. And, sadly, the mainstream media is in lockstep with all of this, not only reflecting but also directing the culture in their attempt to ruin the United States.

Today, we can see what has happened in the cities, the universities, and the streets of the U. S. Scripture describes it: "Your country is desolate, your cities burned with fire; your fields are being stripped by foreigners right before you."[35] That quote reads like a figurative description of our nation during America's spiritual decline, when it is estimated that between eight to ten million "foreigners" have crossed our southern border in the last four years.

Some illegals have come to America seeking a better life, but we have no way of knowing how many came as terrorists or as criminals. In addition, over 150 universities in the U. S. have recently had demonstrations showing support for Hamas, but displaying hatred for Israel and Jews. Antisemitism has become rampant in universities nationwide.

Even the leader of our country in 2024, President Joe Biden, displayed his support for an aspect of the woke agenda by declaring Easter Sunday to be "Trans Day of Visibility." Where was God in the midst of this happening? Obviously, He could see what was occurring and displayed His control. He raised up a man to become our reforming president and protected him when two attempts were made on his life. Then most of the people of our nation, who recognized the need for change, elected Donald J. Trump to be our next president. As even President Trump has acknowledged, God kept him alive to take our nation back and to make America a great nation again.

Like all of us, President Trump has his faults, but as noted, God can choose whomever he wishes to be in authority, and it looks like

Trump is God's man for the season in the U. S. Only he has the will to reverse ungodly laws, to return public education back to the control of parents instead of the big city unions that have adopted "sexually liberalized ideas," and to close the border to stop the illegal flood of immigration jeopardizing our nation.

As our new president and his people are reclaiming our culture and doing everything in their power to take back our land, despite the dangers that entails to both themselves and their families, the least we Christians can do is to take up the task as well. We can't continue being afraid of the secular left or fear possible misquotes from the press or vilification by special interest groups or threats from the radicals. For "God is our refuge and strength, an ever-present help in trouble. Therefore, we will not fear. . . . The Lord Almighty is with us; the God of Jacob is our fortress."[36]

However, that brings us to the seventh reason we should think through our beliefs: We are in a spiritual battle for the existence of our nation! So, what is behind all the polarization and discord in America. Although the defeat of Satan and all he stands for was begun through the death and resurrection of Christ, his final defeat awaits the time when he is banished into hell as set forth in Revelation 20:10.

In the meantime, however, Satan still exercises control (which people have chosen to give him by defying God) as the ruler or "prince of this world." Satan has power and authority in the world and uses all manner of evil against Christ and the church. Satan is permitted to do his work by blinding the minds of non-Christians and deceiving them in order to control their lives: "The god of this age has blinded the minds of unbelievers, so that they cannot see the light of the gospel that displays the glory of Christ, who is the image of God."[37]

But, God is providentially watching over his people, preserving and providing for his creation, and ruling over the universe and earth. God has complete control and authority, for He is sovereign, so the events of history happen only as He allows. There are times when he directly intervenes to accomplish his purposes and to reveal himself to people. But until the time when history is fulfilled, He limits his supreme power and rule in the world. Of course, this self-limitation is only temporary, for God has already set the time when He will destroy Satan and all evil. (See Revelation 19-20)

Thus, Satan exercises considerable control while evil is rampant in the world. In other words, there is a supernatural battle in the world against God and His people. Satan the evil leader, his cohorts the demons, and his followers the unbelievers, have always ridiculed God's people. But, as Christians face opposition and persecution, they must remember "to put on the full armor of God, so that you can take your stand against the devil's schemes. For our struggle is not against flesh and blood, but against the rulers, against the authorities, against the powers of this dark world and against the spiritual forces of evil in the heavenly realms."[38]

Satan is a strategist whose aim is to slow down or stop God's long-range intentions for America to spread the gospel worldwide until He returns. That is the underlying reason God's enemies are fighting tooth and nail to stop President Trumps reform efforts. They are vigorously using all their resources to try to prevent good policies and laws from being enforced in our nation.

These are wicked people who support things such as all sorts of demonstrations to cause civil unrest and evil doings such as setting fire to our cities which will wreck and destabilize our nation. The "powers of this dark world" are the spiritual forces of evil that influence and control ungodly people by blinding their minds so they do these things that oppose God's plans and intentions. Scripture says that "they who forsake the law praise the wicked; but such as keep the law contend with them. Evil men understand not judgment; but they that seek the Lord understand all things."[39]

Thus, regarding the activities of America's leaders, those who oppose the betterment of our society frequently attack people such as Trump and his administration as they attempt to reform America. That's also why it's in the best interests of a society or a nation for the righteous rather than the wicked to flourish and hold power. For "when the righteous are in authority, the people rejoice; but when the wicked beareth rule, the people mourn."[40] Importantly, when leaders rule with justice, it promotes a country's stability and success. In other words, the stability of a nation itself depends on openness to the revelation of God's Word.

## A NOTE ABOUT
## THE WINDOW OF OPPORTUNITY TRILOGY

*A Reasonable Faith* was first published with *A Personal Grief* as a two-book volume in 1991. Recently, after prayer, I decided to reissue both books as part of a "Window of Opportunity Trilogy," along with another book, *A Perilous Time*, with release of all three books scheduled in 2025. The second to eleventh chapters of this book are the original chapters as they first appeared with minimal change.

# 2

# IS IT WRONG TO DOUBT
# OR TO QUESTION?

Some Christians distrust virtually all use of reason or evidences to encourage faith. Why? Because they've been told it is wrong to doubt or to question; doubting or questioning is comparable to spiritual insubordination. Consequently, many people are afraid to admit they have religious uncertainties. Not wanting to invite scorn, these men and women just swallow their doubts. This is one reason large numbers of people either give up on Christianity or look to unconventional religions for answers. Lloyd Ogilve writes:

> The aching problem, both inside and outside the church, is agnosticism. Many people "just don't know" what they think or believe in response to the awesome questions of life. Most of them are afraid to ask and even more frightened that they may be asked and be unable to answer. At the same time, they are troubled by easy answers and pat phrases that do not stand up to authentic spiritual and intellectual honesty. "Click words,"esoteric jargon, and flip theories do not satisfy when life falls apart or tragedy strikes. There are far too few opportunities for Christians and honest inquirers to ask questions that have been lurking beneath the surface and to get straight-arrow answers.[1]

During certain periods in the course of history, men and women dared not communicate their uncertainties concerning religious matters; skepticism carried the death penalty. Alan Richardson writes that Christian philosophy was especially neglected "in an age in which the state orders all its subjects to he baptized in infancy and sends to the stake anyone who ventures to express religious doubts."[2]

Although skeptics are not sent to the stake today, there is very often a low-keyed rejection of those with questioning minds. In her article, "The Heresy of Simple Faith," Maurene Fell Pierson observes that one of "the damaging aspects of this heretical [simple] faith is its subtle persecution of those who do not want its product: these persons are variously labded as atheistic, impious, irreverent, insensitive, and insincere."[3]

In my experience, the low-keyed rejection by some Christians of those who question is very subtle indeed. For example, as a young person I once asked a Bible teacher a question about a possible conflict between science and the Bible. In a tone of voice which indicated to me that such questions would not be tolerated, the teacher answered my question by stating emphatically that one must simply believe such matters by "faith alone!"

My teacher was letting me know he felt it was impious and lacking reverence for God for me to ask such questions. Of course, the teacher didn't have to actually call me an atheist or say I was insensitive or insincere. His tone of voice and manner were enough to squelch any questions I needed to ask. He didn't realize, however, that I was simply looking for rational grounds for accepting Christianity.

Many Christians assume the only thing that separates man from God is man's own corruption or sinfulness. The prevailing attitude is that human thought processes are so corrupted by sin that people cannot come to know God except through "faith alone." Philosophy is regarded as something men and women do in order to postpone or avoid faith; thus there is subtle persecution of those who express spiritual uncertainties or doubts.

In a similar vein, Edward John Carnell (1919-1967) writes that some churchmen insist that salvation entails a submission to the authority of the church, not to the dictates of reason:

> Some may rise to a final defense by asserting that it is our religious *duty* to submit to God's representative, whether we understand the reasons or not; for faith is a venture, a leap of the will in the face of paradox and objective uncertainty. To look for evidences is a sign of unbelief. Any delay will only increase our chances of losing eternal happiness."[4]

Carnell emphasizes that this idea is a "specious claim." God's children should never expect men and women to commit themselves without reasonable grounds. Christians are responsible to show others that "Christ's gospel is consistent with the claims of man's fourfold environment, [whether] physical, rational, esthetic, moral or spiritual."[5]

The belief that "any delay will only increase our chances of losing eternal happiness" results in high pressure evangelism and in questioning the value or the legitimacy of Christian philosophy. Christians are led to feel that it is their obligation to show doubters they should quickly turn aside from reason and walk the path of faith. Historic Christian faith, however, is committed to the concept of *objective truth*.

For example, Paul observes (in dealing with the objective reality of the resurrection): "If Christ be not raised, your faith is vain; . . . We are of all men most miserable. But now is Christ risen from the dead" (I Cor. 15:17-20 KJV). It is also clear from elsewhere in the new testament that Paul never made what is called "a simple presentation of the gospel." Of course, he communicated as simply and as clearly as he could, but he states in Acts 20:27 KJV: "I have not shunned to declare unto you all the counsel of God." In other words Paul took the time to proclaim *all* the truth of the Christian faith. Likewise, we can do the same today.

Of course, doubt, in the face of adequate information, can be a smoke screen covering spiritual rebellion. But all intellectual problems are not necessarily the result of bad motives. Some questions result from the quest for a fuller understanding. Great numbers of men and women honestly search for answers and would gladly accept Christianity if only their doubts could be removed. For example, Jay Kesler writes about a college professor who expressed sincere questions about Christianity:

> Non-Christians aren't always people in angry, sarcastic, argumentative rebellion against God. I find many like that professor, wanting to believe but not seeing that as possible. For them, its important first to show that God is believable, that there is a good basis for accepting as genuine what Christ said. And perhaps they have special questions that need to be answered; this professor was a scientist and needed to be shown (probably by other scientists; through books) that there was no necessary contradiction between science and a belief in God.[6]

This college professor had encountered data which did not seem to fit. He needed clarification that the findings of science and Christianity are not necessarily opposed. Christianity could only be true to him if it could be placed into some rational relationship to all that he knew and had to live with in the external world.

Shouldn't this be true, isn't it true, of all of us. The professor was not attempting to avoid faith or to be disrespectful to God; he was simply looking for answers with which he could live. J. B. Phillips explains:

> Many men and women today are living, often with inner dissatisfaction, without any faith in God at all. This is not because they are particularly wicked or selfish or, as the old-fashioned would say, "godless," but because they have not found with their adult minds a God big enough to "account for" life, big enough to "fit in with" the new scientific age, big enough to command their highest admiration and respect, and consequently their willing cooperation.[7]

The human mind is endowed with an insatiable hunger for rational answers to questions about life; man's deepest needs cannot be satisfied unless his fundamental questions are answered. This is clearly true even for believers. Have you ever tried to explain the death of a loved one to someone who had no real understanding of the problem of evil and the Christian response? Consequently, doubt can be a prelude to spiritual truth; the seeker of truth can use his uncertainties as a motivation to find honest answers. As Peter Abelard (1079-1142) points out, "By doubting we are led to inquire, and by inquiry we perceive the truth."[8]

When non-Christians search for meaning and truth, the last thing they need is for Christians to pronounce judgment upon their doubts. Church should be a place, not where an unbeliever's doubts and questions are shunned, but where such problems receive sympathetic attention. When Christians dismiss the intellectual difficulties of non-Christians as if they do not exist, seekers of truth are left with plaguing doubts as to whether Christianity really makes sense.

The problem is complicated by the fact that some Christians have never practiced philosophical thinking; their faith has been acquired by a type of untested assent. Faith comes easily; it never occurs to them to doubt. These believers fail to realize that numerous men and women need for them to know Christian philosophy. Without a Christian answer, many people are left defenseless against the false philosophy of unconventional religious. C. S. Lewis observes, "Good philosophy must exist, if for no other reason, because bad philosophy needs to be answered."[9]

"Faith alone" is no longer meaningful in our world with its endless variety of religions; unbelievers need more than a mere testimony of a subjective experience as a standard for choosing between religions. In our modern world, men and women from many religious backgrounds testify to experiences in which they claim to have found ultimate truth. Josh McDowell writes, "The Mormons talk about the burning in their heart; those in Eastern religions will talk about the peace and tranquility they receive; others will admit to a new joy or happiness."[10]

Christian philosophy is needed to critique these non-Christian outlooks, to point out various problems with views that fail on philosophical grounds. Terry Miethe proclaims the many merits of Christian philosophy:

> Christian philosophy can help the believer and the unbeliever to know the evidence for a Christian world view, to better understand the essence of the faith, to expose claims against the faith that are not true and to show, though all the evidence may not be in, that the Christian position is a credible intellectual position as against the counterclaims of its opponents. All of these are extremely important to the individual Christian and to the church. Christians, therefore, must be good philosophers.[11]

Jesus has called Christians to be the salt of the earth. Among other things this means believers should offer alternatives to the ideas which exist around them. It is a grave failure of Christians to close off the possibilities for non-Christians to distinguish between truth and falsehood. If God's people won't stand up for the truth, others are left defenseless to resist the pressure of false religions. Christians should help mankind to see that great differences exist between Christianity and other forms of religion. The complete picture makes sense only with the Christian point of view. Other ways of looking at the world full short—the pieces of the puzzle don't quite fit.

Is it really wrong to doubt or to question? Is it contrary to the teaching of Scripture to search for answers or seek for truth? The Word of God proclaims, "And you will seek Me and find Me, when you search for Me with all your heart" (Jer. 29:13). The word "heart" is often used in the Bible to refer to the mind or the human ability to reason. Turning to the Bible, we joyfully discover it is never wrong to think through or reason our beliefs, to search for God with our whole soul and our entire being. As Edward John Carnell points out, "Faith is a whole-souled response to critically tested evidences. To believe in defiance of such evidences would outrage the image of God in man."[12]

# 3

# IS IT ENOUGH TO JUST BELIEVE?

A familiar segment from Charles Lutwidge Dodgson's (1832-1898) *Through the Looking Glass* presents a common view of religious faith, the view that faith is contrary to reason:

> "I can't believe *that*!" said Alice. "Can't you?" the Queen said in a pitying tone. "Try again: draw a long breath, and shut your eyes." Alice laughed. "There's no use trying," she said. "One *can't* believe impossible things." "I daresay you haven't had much practice," said the Queen. "Why, sometimes I've believed as many as six impossible things before breakfast."[1]

When Dodgson, writing under the pseudonym Lewis Carroll, created the piece, he was undoubtedly aware of its theological implications. The passage promotes the act of belief rather than any real object of belief, believing is the most important thing.

The ludicrous nature of this viewpoint is obvious—believing something will not make it true! Josh McDowell writes, "Belief will not create fact. I may believe with all my heart that I want it to snow tomorrow, but this will not guarantee snow. Or I may believe that my rundown old car is really a new Rolls Royce, but my belief won't change the fact."[2]

Truth is completely independent of belief. Without a rational basis for faith, the believer would be in company with the White Queen in *Through the Looking Glass* who could believe "as many as six impossible things before breakfast." C. E. M. Joad observes there can be no believing that the intellect cannot justify:

> Men have spoken of "the will to believe," a phrase popularized by William James. But divorced from reason, the dictates of the will have no authority and carry no conviction. One might just as well will to believe X as will to believe Y. The fact that one does believe X is, on this view, evidence of nothing but the fact that one wills to believe X. The willing of the belief has, then, no bearing upon the truth of that which the belief asserts."[3]

Unreflective acceptance of beliefs is impossible for many non-Christians. These men and women crave logical guarantees of the credibility of Christian faith. When searchers voice their questions or uncertainties concerning the objective and factual truth of the gospel, however, Christians frequently admonish them to "just believe" or to "just have faith." In the name of "faith," some believers discourage seekers from investigating the truth claims of Christianity.

Resorting to proof texts, "pat answers," and mechanical forms of witnessing, certain Christians emphasize schemes which tend to obscure real reasoning. When the results of such efforts are small, the blame is attributed to the hardness of the hearts of the hearers. Instead, could it be some of God's people have forgotten the Bible's command to always be "ready to make a defense to everyone who asks you to give an account for the hope that is in you" (1 Peter 3:15)?

Thus, M. Vernon Davis of Midwestern Baptist Seminary of Kansas City writes:

> Someone has said that Christianity is much like great music. It really does not need a strong defense so much as it needs a good performance. A person is more likely to become convinced by seeing a demonstration of the "the real thing," than by hearing the most persuasive arguments for its truth.[4]

According to Davis, men and women should accept the message of Christianity merely on the basis of the testimony of the committed lives of Christians.

While it is certainly very important for Christians to show non-Christians "the real thing," that is, lives that are authentic and really alive; to somehow indicate that this "real thing" can or should be separate from knowledge and a reasonable faith is ultimately devastating to biblical Christianity. And, to relate "the real thing," to "a good performance" is misleading at best! After all, a "performance," as in acting, is most often only a counterfeit of the truly real. Mormons reportedly live very committed moral lives as do many other non-Christians. The question remains: "How does one distinguish between 'daily walks' if not by reason and objective historical evidence?"

Why do some folks deny that argument for the truth of the gospel can be helpful in leading others to belief in God? Throughout history, there has been a seesaw relationship concerning the faith and reason concepts. A balanced relationship between the two factors has seldom existed. During some periods, faith has been overly elevated; during others, reason has been greatly promoted. Gary Habermas, in Terry Miethe's *A Christians Guide to Faith and Reason*, observes:

While philosophers should be students of the history of thought, we never seem to learn the error of countering one incorrect school of thought by advocating its exact reverse. In other words, we too often respond to one movement by encouraging the pendulum to swing too far in the opposite direction. Trends in philosophy verify this back- and-forth movement.

Miethe and Habermas affirm the "equal importance of both the facts of the gospel and one's personal faith-commitment to them." Faith and reason are both important; yet Christians often devalue one or the other, "leading to extreme positions that endanger the very nature of the gospel. To unduly elevate faith has led to various forms of the 'leap of faith,' while the over-elevation of reason often leads to various rationalistic errors."[5]

Contributing to the latest swing of the faith and reason pendulum were "rationalistic errors" of the Middle Ages. Reacting against the excessive promotion of reason in that era, many theologians turned completely away from natural theology and focused on means such as religious experience and emotional feelings to foster a belief in God.

Numerous church leaders note that modern evangelicalism nursed on emotionalism and gospel music has been little more than a mood-centered movement. Calvin Miller writes:

Christianity has too often had a merely emotional approach to worship. In the wake of neo-Pentecostalism, we have been prone to step up our emotions while gearing down our intellects, which can produce Christians infatuated with feeling their faith rather than knowing it. New converts often, become satisfied with a gelatinous "chummyism" that shakes with fervor but is without substance. This naivete leaves us powerless to answer the skeptics. Ours are desperate times.[6]

Oliver Barclay maintains "the current culture of the Western world is tending to put feelings so much before thinking that it has in some circles become hard to defend Christian thinking at all."[7] Many Christians today feel intellectual matters are irrelevant in the pursuit of Christ—emotionalism is more important than thinking about the basis for one's faith. It is not easy to convince such people that their faith should consist of more than good "feelings."

According to Francis Schaeffer, individuals can cause quite an uproar in modern Christendom just by mentioning that true faith is based on more than emotional considerations: "To say (as a Christian should) that only the faith which believes God on the basis of knowledge is true faith, is to say something which causes an explosion in the modern world."[8]

Deeply ingrained in the minds of many present day Christians is the idea that reason and knowledge are useless as evangelical tools. Therefore, Terry Miethe notes that a lack of emphasis on knowledge is apparent in the Sunday schools and the preaching in many churches:

One might think from observing many Sunday schools, the lessons presented in them and the way we prepare for these lessons, that we in the church are unconcerned about Christians being educated in the faith, and that we are apparently against biblical/theological education altogether. [In addition], look at the preaching in many, many churches. We have heard so often, "We must preach the whole counsel of God" meaning we must preach all that He has commanded us (Matt. 28:20). But preaching the whole counsel of God is so very different than the kind that never does, in fact, give people the bibical meat necessary to mature in their understanding of Christian commentment. Preachers *must* see the relationship between faith and reason and must be willing to spend long hours in biblical study."[9]

Man is a thinking as well as a feeling creature. Because his faith must be thought through as well as lived out, he must exercise critical judgment in the context of his beliefs. When ministers and lay Christians begin to recognize this import-

ant kinship of faith and knowledge, they will no longer find it necessary to ask non-Christians to "just believe." Obeying the Bible's command to be ready always "to make a defense to everyone who asks you to give an account for the hope that is in you" (1 Peter 3:15), Christians will not expect people to commit themselves without reasonable grounds. In this regard, F. R. Beattie observes:

> Christianity is either everything for mankind, or nothing. It is either the highest certainty or the greatest delusion But if Christianity be everything for mankind, it is important for every man to be able to give a good reason for the hope that is in him in regard to the eternal verities of the Christian faith. To accept these verities in an unthinking way, or to receive them simply on authority, is not enough for an intelligent and stable faith.[10]

Today, there is desperate need for God's people to stabilize the faith and reason pendulum. For hundreds of years, Christians have been swinging to and fro, placing too much emphasis either on belief or on knowledge, seldom balancing these extremes. It is very important that Christians refrain from over reacting again.

Habermas and Miethe warn that Philosophical truth is frequently a delicate balance of extreme views:

> We must be ever so careful not to elevate reason so that faith suffers, or vice-versa. To suppress the biblical view of either faith or facts can have an important affect on the gospel . . . The elevation of the leap of faith has progressed to the very point of denying the facts of the gospel while the elevation of reason and the need for Cartesian certainty leads to skepticism. To balance both facts and faith is to be both more biblical and more practical.[11]

True faith is a "whole-souled" response. Nels F. S. Ferre writes, "those needs of whole response must naturally include the needs of the mind for truth, of the heart for high emotion, and of the will for right and satisfying action."[12] For proper conversion to happen, the total personality must be yielded to God.

In the parable of the sower (Mark 4), Jesus tells the story of the farmer who sowed seed in different kinds of soil. The soils can represent differing responses men and women make to God. In these verses Jesus first illustrates some responses that are not genuine "conversion" experiences.

Three improper responses are described: the intellectual, the emotional, and the volitional. Without the involvement of the emotions and the will, the purely intellectual response is comparable to the seed that "fell beside the road." Jesus tells about the person who has head knowledge but lacks spiritual insight or understanding.

Minus the assistance of the intcllect and the will, the solely emotional response is likened to the seed that "fell on the rocky ground." Christ pictures the individual who has some shallow emotional experience with "God," but possesses no "root" or "depth."

Unassisted by the emotions and the intellect, the purely volitional response is akin to the seed that "fell among the thorns." Jesus describes the man or woman who makes a "decision" but fails to live up to it because the cares of the world choke his commitment as seeds are choked when planted among thorns.

These responses do *not* represent true Christian conversion. Commenting on the parable of the sower, Paul Little notes that Christ indirectly warns us in the story against the use of evangelistic techniques which could produce those abortive results:

> At the outset, we must concede the possibility of manipulating human emotions in some circumstances. And we would have to admit that some evangelists consciously or unconsciously play on the emotions of their audiences with death-bed stories, histrionic performances, and other devices. Our Lord, in the parable of the sower, implicitly warns against merely stirring the emotions in evangelism.[13]

In this same vein, Richard Dugan observes, "Unfortunately, salvation has been reduced by some to a "plan" or "formula." But praying even all the right words with the proper inflection will not touch God if it is not from the heart and the expression of the whole heart."[14]

Finally, in the parable of the sower, Jesus describes the whole-souled response of true faith; the proper reaction of mind to truth, of heart to emotion, and of will to action. Genuine Christian conversion is comparable to the seed that "fell into the good soil" bringing forth fruit thirty, sixty, or a hundredfold—a total and permanent reorientation of a life.

God has said we will find him when we search for him with *all* our heart (Jer. 29:13). Involved are our minds, our emotions, and our wills. Since a proper conversion can be aborted by neglect of just one of these faculties, it is extremely important that all factors be stressed.

Should we stop using our minds and "just believe"? No! There can be no believing that the intellect cannot justify. As Edward John Carnell points out:

> Whatever else faith may be, it is at least a "resting of the mind in the sufficiency of evidences. " The extent of this sufficiency is measured by a cool and dispassionate use of reason. An upright man cannot violate the rational environment; he cannot believe logical contradictions. If a dispassionate use of reason assures him that he has no money in his pocket, all the existential heat in the world cannot induce him to act on the firm assurance that he is rich.[15]

Accordingly, the most urgent task of contemporary Christians is to express a credible faith for modern mankind, a faith so stated that men and women can be convinced in their minds. Returning one last time to *Through the Looking Glass*, it will not suffice to take the White Queen's strange advice, "Try again: draw a long breath, and shut your eyes."

# 4

# IS CHRISTIANITY JUST A PSYCHOLOGICAL CRUTCH?

A famous line from Karl Marx (1818-1883), "Religion is the opiate of the masses," captures the essence of a common view of Christian faith. Religion is seen as an attractive intoxicant or drug for weak people who can't cope with their future on their own. Overpowered by the harsh realities of life, men and women use Christianity just like alcohol or drugs to survive in this difficult world.

According to the viewpoint, a religious person operates strictly from emotion to handle his needs and weaknesses; Christianity is a subjective experience that has no objective reality. People believe in God because they want to believe, not because they have a rational basis.

In connection with that idea, a parallel expression is often heard, "I don't need religion," as if the basis of Christianity resulted from the religious needs of mankind. The root of the statement is the assumption that man invents God out of the pressures of his human fears and weaknesses. Christianity is seen as a psychological crutch for the emotionally weak.

To support the psychological crutch view, major critics of religion such as Nietzsche (1844-1900), Russel (1877-1970), Sartre (1905-1980), Marx (1818-1883), and Freud (1856-1939) have set forth various theories of the origin of religion. Although the theories differ in points of detail, they all contain the common thread or idea that religion owes its origin and its influence to the psychological needs of mankind. Kenneth Boa and Larry Moody, authors of *I'm Glad You Asked*, write that skeptics such as Marx and Freud have protrayed religion as something for the emotionally weak:

> Marx saw the problem as economic; religion is the carrot on a stick used by the upper classes to keep the lower classes from revolting. The masses were kept in tow with the promise of a better existence in the next life if they persevered now. Freud and others related religion to the fear that comes from contending with natural forces. According to Freud, man invented God to help him deal with the dangers and unknowns of life. Now that man is more sophisticated and less superstitious, there is little need for God [1]

The fact is we all *do* have profound spiritual needs that only God can meet; belief in God is related to the basic human drive toward meaning in life. Human beings possess an inborn, almost irrepressible desire to discover life's ultimate meaning. In my own case, I had long felt a need for meaning and truth, a need for God. Yet this need was suppressed until the tragedy of my daughter's death made the need se great it could no longer be ignored. Without spiritual answers, my life seemed meaningless. I was desperate for truth; otherwise, I couldn't bear to go on living.

Seeking answers to basic questions about our existence is not particularly a sign of weakness, however. In *How to Respond to a Skeptic*, Lewis Drummond and Paul Baxter observe:

Great thinkers like Rudolph Otto, C. A. Campbell, Anselm, and a host of others contend that the universal religious instinct is far from weakness or unrealistic, as the skeptic charges. Actually they realize that to seek meaning and God is to face reality "as we find it."[2]

True faith is not the invention of cowards or the weak, but the unfailing resource of courageous men and women who have dared to face reality.

But, if we all have deep spiritual needs that only God can fill, why is it that some men and women do not feel this drive toward meaning? The answer involves the fact that people find themselves at different places in relation to the basic human need for meaning and truth. Clark Pinnock states:

Obviously there are many who do face up to the issue and conduct a search for meaning. But then there are others on whom the question has not yet settled in full force. If life has been good to them, they probably have some personal goals, in their job or marriage, which give them enough satisfaction that the question of deeper meaning seems remote. Unfortunately, however, the realities of life have a way of ganging up on a person with shallow assumptions. Something almost always comes along to shatter the dream and raise the issue of meaning for them.[3]

Enjoying the superficial pleasures of life, some people aren't interested in searching for answers. Because a non-Christian can find temporary satisfaction in family, work, money, and other externals, the issue of the meaning of life may be distant. But that contentment depends upon circumstances. When things go badly, such happiness fails. Pinnock adds:

Happiness based on worldly security alone is endlessly vulnerable to the "slings and arrows of outrageous fortune" which may come in the form of illness or inflation or the loss of a loved one. There are all manner of threats to the meaning of our lives both internal and external which can conspire to destroy it if it is not grounded.[4]

The trouble with "happiness based on worldly security alone" is that it always proves to be a mere shadow; contentment grounded solely on temporal values is continually subject to the "slings and arrows" of life. Hardships and tragedies of our existence serve to remind us, however, of our need for deeper meaning and purpose, of our real need for God. Pinnock concludes, "The goodness and worthwhileness of life will always be threatened until it is located within the vision of an intelligible and purposive order of significance and meaning that cannot be shaken."[5]

When the "slings and arrows of outrageous fortune" strike, crippled people need a solid foundation that cannot be shaken, a cure rather than a crutch. Jesus said, "Therefore everyone who hears these words of Mine, and acts upon them, may be compared to a wise man, who built his house upon the rock" (Matt. 7:24). Instead of offering a religious crutch, Christianity proffers a true remedy, a relationship with Jesus Christ, the rock of life. Nevertheless, it has been noted that sufferers generally lean on a variety of false crutches rather than on Christ. Charles Swindoll writes:

I've worked with people for more than twenty-five years. And I've seen them in the worst kind of crises. It has been my observation that people usually do one four things when they're faced with information like this. I think of these responses as common crutches on which people lean. Popular though these four crutches may be, escapism, cynicism, humanism, and supernaturalism do not provide any sense of ultimate relief and satisfaction. They leave the victim in quicksand, more confused than at the beginning.[6]

The first crutch is "escapism." People often try to avoid the harsh realities of life by running away either emotionally or literally. Keeping busy through work, travel, play, or other activity, people refuse to think about their situation, to let reality really sink in. Others escape into an unreal world of drug or alcohol induced numbness to the unpleasant aspects of life. And tragically, some lose the will to go on. In a final bid to escape the pain, they take their own lives.

Second, there is the crutch of "cynicism." Preoccupied with the troubles of life, many people grow dark and cold within. Often they spend the balance of their lives in disillusionment, resentment, and bitterness against God. Dwelling on their suffering, men and women become victims of their own lack of forgiveness. Permanently angry at God, they refuse to accept his help and his love.

Third, others turn to "humanism." By directing their thoughts toward humanitarian goals, these individuals defend themselves from serious reflection about life and death. They assume that if they live a moral life, love others, and do good, their eternity, if there is one, will turn out all right. In other words, they think they are "hedging their bet." Hence, some people fail to come to terms with the real truth of what could be learned from their troubles. And, sadly, their real need for God remains unmet.

The fourth crutch is "supernaturalism." Trying desperately to cope with their painful existence, others turn to the world of the occult—to the realm of witchcraft, magic, wizardry, satanism, or astrology. Or they turn to mediums in their search for info from the other world. Dealing in the dangerous sphere of demonic powers, these individuals often reject sources of true knowledge of the God who gives true peace.

Peace is the longing of every human bean, but mankind can find true fulfillment and peace only in God. Christ alone holds the answers to our questions, our search. He is the final resting place of our worries, our tragedies, our griefs, and our cares. Jesus said, "Come to Me, all who are weary and heavy-laden, and I will give you rest" (Matt. 11:28). People can seek peace and security in many different ways, but only in Christ can they find true rest. Paul Little observes:

> The human spirit can never be satisfied "by bread alone," by material things. We have been made for God and can never find rest until we rest in Him. It is very moving to hear the testimony of those who have restlessly searched for years and have finally found peace in Christ. The current rise in narcotic addiction, alcoholism, and sex obsession are vain hopes of gaining the peace which is in Christ alone.[7]

Without belief in God, the non-Christian must logically accept death as his final end. He believes the realm of time and space are the only reality; thus, he considers the life of growth to death within that order to be the only existence and human life to be meaningless. There is ultimately nothing to hope for or to believe in. But Christianity offers an unending, eternal purpose for life. Harry Blamires comments:

> Christianity is therefore a very remarkabk religion indeed. In the first place it says, "There is a state of being beyond time and space where God dwells eternally." But it does not go on to say, "So this life here in the natural order is not all that important." No, instead of that, Christianity goes on

to say, "But this world of space and time has been visited by God himself. He became one of us. He demonstrated indeed that our passing physical life here can be involved with his eternal life beyond and above the universe."[8]

Wonderfully, the supernatural reality "that our passing physical life here can be involved with his eternal life" has enabled me to rejoice even in the midst of storm, to transcend difficult circumstances. In his twenties, my son David was involved in a terrible car accident where he suffered a broken back injury. Although situations like that can be difficult to cope with in an earthly sense, during that time I experienced an inner peace that defies natural understanding: "the peace of God" (Phil. 4:7). Of course, as a mother, I was very concerned about my son; yet God's grace was sufficient for me.

Thus, whatever the test or the trial, Christianity has given to my life a deep sense of purpose and meaning, for now and for eternity. As Nels F. S. Ferre points out, "Blessedness is living now in the peace beyond this world which we know shall transform all suffering into endless praise."[9]

In Christianity we have the actual entrance of God into the human scene in the person of Jesus Christ, and this entrance is verifiable by means of his bodily resurrection. As Barry Wood observes: "There is historical documentation of his life, death, and bodily resurrection."[10] This "object" of our faith is not just some fabrication of man's mind, but a physical, historical reality. Jesus Christ is really "there."

# 5

# ARE ALL RELIGIONS TRUE?

Christianity, according to some people, is just one of an assortment of religions which are equally right or correct. Although there are some technical distinctions within this variety of religions, all of them are, in essence, considered true. Thus, when Christians make an exclusive claim to the truth of Christianity, that position is often met with anger at what some perceive as an intolerant posture.

Why do so many people think it unlikely Christianity could contain final truth? In our country under the principle of religious toleration, all religious systems are guaranteed freedom of expression and equal treatment under the law. With the principle of equal toleration has come the idea that no religion has exclusive claims to truth, the implication that equal toleration means equal validity.

It is one thing, however, to protect the right of every religious person to follow the dictates of his conscience without fear of persecution and quite another to say that opposing convictions are all true. We must recognize the difference between equal toleration under the law and equal validity according to truth. Paul Little explains the difference between toleration and truth:

We live in an age in which tolerance is a key word. Tolerance, however, must be clearly understood. (Truth, by its very nature, is intolerant of error.) If two plus two is four, the total cannot at the same time be 23. But one is not regarded as intolerant because he disagrees with this answer and maintains that the only correct answer is four. The same principle applies in religious matters. One must be tolerant of other points of view and respect their right to be held and heard. He cannot, however, be forced in the name of tolerance to agree that all points of view, including those that are mutually contradictory, are equally valid. Such a position is nonsense.[1]

Religious tolerance today has reached the point where it is no longer a virtue but a vice, a cruel casualness to truth. It is as if we said to a blind man sitting on the edge of a precipice, "It doesn't matter which way you move. All routes lead to the same goal." Equally, no kindness is displayed if we tell someone that all religions lead to God.

Before becoming a Christian, I had often wondered if all religions were correct or if only one was true. Reading Christian apologist C. S. Lewis, I discovered that Christianity emphasized objective truth: real history, people, places, and events. If it is true, it is true for everybody. If it is untrue, it is not true for anybody. Jesus said, "I am the way, and the truth, and the life; no one comes to the Father, but through Me" (John 14:6). If Jesus said He is the only way to God, and some other religion claimed to be another way to God, then either Jesus is wrong or the other religion is wrong. They cannot both be right.

It is illogical to assert all religions are relatively true. How can all religions lead to God when they are so different? We can see this by considering the five great world religions: Buddhism, Hinduism,

Islam, Judaism, and Christianity. Religions of the East such as Buddhism and Hinduism have a markedly different conception of God from Christianity.

First, making no ultimate distinction between their god and the universe, Eastern religions teach that god is all and all is god: you are god; I am god; the grass is god; the dirt is god; the insects are god; everything is god. According to the Bible, however, God is not the same as his creation: "In the beginning God created the heavens and the earth" (Gen. 1:1).

Second, viewing god as one with the universe, religions of the East see god as ultimately impersonal, as an "it," but Christianity teaches that God is personal: "For God so loved the world, that He gave His only begotten Son" (John 3:16). The God of Christianity has a capacity to love the world.

Third, the impersonal god of Eastern thought cannot have any interest in mankind, but the Christian God is intimately concerned in the affairs of man. Jesus said, "Take My yoke upon you, and learn from me, for I am gentle and humble in heart; and you shall find rest for your souls" (Matt. 11:29).

As we have seen, the God of Christianity is not the same as the impersonal god or gods of the Eastern religions. But what about the Islamic concept of God? In Islam, we have a God closer to the Christian concept, a god who is personal and transcendent, or separate from his creation. Are Muslims worshiping the same God as the One revealed in the Bible? In a philosophical sense there can only be one Supreme Being. But the characteristics of this Supreme Being are markedly different in Muslim teaching than in Christianity.

There are three significant reasons it is impossible Muslims and Christians are worshiping the same God. First of all, the sources of authority for the two religions are different. Muslims accept the Koran as their final source of authority and believe that the Bible contains errors. The Bible claims to be the inerrant Word of God, the final authority on all matters.

Second, the Koran portrays a different God from Christianity. The Islamic concept of God is called "Allah" and within his nature there is only one person. Christian Scripture explains that there is one God who has eternally existed in three persons—the Father, the Son, and the Holy Spirit—the doctrine of the Trinity. Islam rejects the Trinity and the New Testament teaching that Jesus is the eternal God, considering him only a prophet. The New Testament reveals, however, that Jesus is "the Son of God" (John 1:34).

Finally, the Islamic religion teaches a different view of salvation. The Koran states that a person can be saved only by his own good deeds: "They whose balances shall be heavy shall be blest. But they whose balances shall be light, they shall lose their soul, abiding in hell forever" (Sura 13:102-104). Yet the Bible discloses that we cannot earn our salvation, for we need a Savior, Jesus Christ, who died to save us from our sins: "Not on the basis of deeds which we have done in righteousness, but according to His mercy" (Titus 3:5).

The Jewish concept of God is closest of all to the Christian. But, again, the sources of authority in Judaism and Christianity are not exactly the same. Even though Jews believe in the Old Testament, most Jews have never accepted that Testament's prophecies relating to the divinity of Jesus Christ or the New Testament's message concerning him. Jewish people are strong unitarians; they believe in only one God and only one Person in the Godhead.

Thus, Jews don't believe their God was the Father of Jesus Christ. Without a belief in the deity of Christ, however, proponents of Judaism must stress salvation by works. But the Bible says that "by grace you have been saved through faith; and that not of yourselves, it is the gift of God, not as a result of works, that no one should boast" (Eph. 2:8-9).

The major difference between Christianity and other world religions is that Christ gives us forgiveness and cleansing as a free gift. In contrast, non-Christian religions essentially teach a "works" system of reaching God or becoming better. As Cliffe Knechtle observes:

> All the other major world religions teach that you must get yourself together. You must pray five times a day, give alms, fast, take a pilgrimage, use a Tibetan prayer wheel, not eat certain foods, observe the sabbath, go to church or live a decent life or one of innumerable other possibilities. Christianity is different. God tells us we will never earn heaven or deserve a right relationship with him. We simply cannot live up to God's standards. Instead, God has taken the initiative. Jesus Christ, the Son of God, died on the cross to take the punishment you and I have earned.[2]

In reaching down to mankind, Christ has done something for us that we could not do for ourselves. No other religion tells how God has taken the initiative to provide for our salvation; other religions are a matter of man struggling to find God. In Christianity God has offered us a free gift: forgiveness and eternal life.

But how should a Christian evaluate other religions? Are other faiths all wrong? Christians do not say other religions are completely false. There are partial truths in every religious tradition, truths that Christianity conserves. Every virtuous thought, every glimmer of light, every word of truth to be found in any religion is part of God's self-disclosure. There is an enormous amount of the moral and the worthy, the beautiful and the good, in other religions. But there are also deep-seated differences. C. S. Lewis points out:

> If you are a Christian, you are free to think that these religions, even the queerest, contain at least some hint of the truth. . . . But being a Christian does mean thinking that where Christianity differs from other religions, Christianity is right and they are wrong. As in arithmetic—there is only one right answer to a sum, and all other answers are wrong; but some of the wrong answers are nearer being right than others.[3]

Christians don't mean other faiths are wrong in the sense that they produce nothing worthy or beautiful. Instead, other religions are wrong as the framework of ultimate, objective belief. Also, insofar as these faiths do not provide the true substance of God's dealings with manknd, they cannot solve the human predicament. Other religions may embody some true awareness of God, but a follower of Jesus must regard Him alone as God's decisive revelation of Himself.

Christians stress the conviction that God has acted decisively in Christ. But Christianity is not stressing some supposed superiority of Christian believers to members of other religions. In the light of the cross, Christians have nothing of which to boast, seeing themselves as sinners, deserving of nothing but condemnation. But they see also that God has acted in grace to bring men to salvation.

In Christianity we are dealing with history. There is plenty of documentary evidence to support the claim that Jesus of Nazareth rose from the dead on the first Easter Day almost 2000 years ago and launched the Christian community.[4] His scattered followers did not claim merely that a corpse had been resuscitated; they believed that almighty God was incarnated as the man Jesus, that he suffered and died on the cross, and that death could not hold him! Christ's resurrection vindicates his claim to deity, his claim to be the way, the truth, and the life. As Josh McDowell notes, no other religion or religious leaders can bring someone to the knowledge of the one true God:

> When it comes to eternal matters, we are going to ask the one who is alive the way out of the predicament. This is not Mohammed, not Confucius, but Jesus Christ. Jesus is unique. He came back from the dead. This demonstrates He is the one whom He claimed to be (Romans 1:4), the unique Son of God and the only way by which a person can have a personal relation ship with the true and living God.[5]

But what should we think about the destiny of those in other religions? We should realize that missionary activity is imperative because Jesus Christ has commanded us to take the gospel to all nations (Matt. 28:19). It is the mandate of our Lord that those who have not heard do hear, that "the gospel be preached in every land and nation, to every tribe and tongue, to every living person. If this mandate were carried out by the church, the question of what happens to those who never heard would be a moot one."[6]

Are all religions true? Christians believe in the uniqueness of Christ because scripture tells us, "There is no other name under heaven that has been given among men, by which we must be saved" (Acts 4:12). Paul Little stresses:

> A Christian cannot be faithful to his Lord and affirm anything else. He is faced with the problem of truth. If Jesus Christ is who He claims to be, then we have the

authoritative word of God Himself on the subject. If He is God and there is no other Saviour, then obviously He is the way to God. Christians could not change this fact by a vote or by anything else.[7]

# 6

# DOES THE BIBLE CONFLICT WITH SCIENCE?

A distinctly contemporary barrier to faith involves the relationship, or apparent conflict, between science and the Bible.[1] Numerous men and women who correctly see that a belief in Christianity is linked to commitment to the truthfulness of the bible are disturbed by the account of creation in Genesis. The bible seems to them to teach that the universe and earth were created very recently in six literal twenty-four hour days and that God created humans in a special act. But that interpretation of the bible apparently conflicts with the widely accepted scientific view that the universe and earth are extremely old and that all of life evolved by natural processes from inanimate matter.[2]

Thus many thoughtful minds are led to question the compatibility of knowledge obtained by scientific investigation of nature and knowledge derived from study of the Holy Bible.

Of course, until modern times, there was little question about the length of the "days" of creation in the bible story. It was popularly assumed that the cosmos was created in six literal twenty-four hour days only a few thousand years ago. Due to scientific study in the nineteenth century, however, it became increasingly clear that the universe was billions of years old. The question of a possible conflict between the bible and science is therefore a comparatively recent problem, presenting a serious obstacle to faith for many individuals.

Although modern people, young and old, are confronted with this tremendous obstruction to belief, the church has overwhelmingly failed, up to this point, to deal in a satisfactory manner with the relationship between the bible and science. Of the three religious approaches to the matter, two are incorrect but vocal, and one is correct but practically silent on this area of considerable concern.

The first approach, the "Liberal" or "Modernist" viewpoint, is unacceptable biblically. As Don Stewart notes, Liberals "teach that a person can accept the biblical teaching about God, heaven, hell, salvation, and etc.. without accepting statements of scripture about historical or scientific matters"[3]

According to this view, often referred to as "limited inerrancy," it is proper to make a distinction between theological and historical or scientific statements. But the bible makes no such distinction, teaching that "All scripture is inspired by God" (2 Tim. 3:16). The bible also testifies that the Word of God is always true: "I, the Lord, speak righteousness declaring things that are upright" (Isa. 45:19). In addition, it is very important to remember that the Bible does not claim to be a textbook of science.

Yet, by advocating an errant scripture, Liberals are, in effect, denying the truthfulness of God's Word and seriously undermining the bible's authority. Consequently, they have put a serious roadblock in the path of many unbelievers who are led to question the truthfulness of Scripture. The historical view of the church is that the bible, from beginning to end, is completely inerrant or infallible.

Stewart points out that inerrancy means "that when all the facts are known, the bible, in the original autographs, will prove itself to be without error in all matters that it covers, including theology, history, science, and all other disciplines of knowledge."[4] He also explains that the biblical doctrine of inerrancy is understood with the following qualifications:

> Inerrancy only covers the original writings of the authors of the bible; it extends to the writings of the different authors, not to the writers themselves; the doctrine of inerrancy allows for the bible to be written in non-scientific descriptions; it also allows for different writers to describe the same events with different details; inerrancy allows for pictorial language and figures of speech; and the doctrine of inerrancy does not demand adherence to the strict rules of grammar. But the important consideration is that the bible is the inspired Word of God and in its original autographs inerrant.[5]

Another approach with serious difficulties regarding the relationship between the bible and science is held by a group calling themselves "creationists" or "creation scientists." Reacting against the Liberal approach, creationists have erred in the opposite direction—whereas the former reject the reliability of the bible in the name of science, the latter seem to reject the validity of science in the name of the bible. Roland Mushat Frye states that creationists, in trying to protect the inerrancy of Scripture, believe in what is called:

> A young-earth theory based upon a strictly literalistic reading of Genesis. These young-earth theories typically can allow no more than 144 hours to the whole process of creation, or, with the digital adjustment by which one day is taken to be a thousand years, they can extend that to

6,000 years. As for the total age of the universe, they allow only a few thousand years, up to a maximum of perhaps 10,000 or 20,000. Basically, that is the time scale with its many implications, which creationism seeks to impose upon our scientific and religious understanding. It differs radically from the long time scale—running into several billion years—for which scientists find abundant evidence in nature. It also differs radically from the understanding of biblical records held by mainstream religion and theology.[6]

Frye stresses that creation-science dogma and strategy are rejected by religious denominations which represent the largest total proportions of Christians in this country. While these mainstream denominations affirm God's creation of the universe, they deny the eccentric interpretation of creation which creation-science seeks to impose.

Davis Young agrees, "Christians have always believed, as they still do, that God created and sustains the entire universe. But many and perhaps most Christians regret, as I do, that the words 'creationists' and 'creationism' are being used today by a relatively small group for very special purposes."[7]

Although creationists are few in number, a minority, they have been extremely vocal in pushing their viewpoint. Edwin Olson observes, "In publications galore, this message [creationism] has been disseminated through religious bookstores all over America. It has been picked up by a diverse readership—pastors, speakers, youth workers, and Sunday school teachers."[8] Even though the creationist message represents a problematic understanding of the relationship between the bible and science, it is heard by many people and creates the false impression that the viewpoint is the only possibility true to the Bible.

However, what is popularly believed by some vocal Christians is not necessarily what the Bible teaches. Young notes that creationists have distorted the findings of nature to gain an accommodation with what they are persuaded is the only possible legitimate interpretation of the Bible:

> They have tried to make nature say things it is not saying. Elsewhere I have documented that creationists have ignored data when convenient and have been very selective in the use of other data. They have attempted to develop a wholly new science. Their wholly new science agrees with their biblical interpretation, but it has almost nothing to do with the facts of the earth, rocks, chemical element distribution, fossils, and so on, except in the most superficial way. Their theory of a young earth and a global-flood catastrophe has been superimposed not only on the bible, but on nature as well. Such an approach to the harmonization of the Bible with nature is no harmonization at all, for it harmonizes by ignoring the real world in which God has placed us.[9]

Creationists have presented their theory before the public as in accord with scripture and nature. People must recognize, however, that this modem young-earth creationism is problematic at best, and furthermore, that creationism, and flood geology have put a serious stumbling block in the way of some unbelievers:

> Although Christ has the power to save unbelievers in spite of our foolishness and poor presentations of the gospel Christians should do all they can to avoid creating unnecessary stumbling blocks to the reception of the gospel Some people who might otherwise be open to the gospel could be completely turned off by flood geology. If

acceptance of Christianity means accepting flood geology, some will not want to become Christians.[10]

The third approach to the question of the relationship between scripture and science is held by "mainstream" Christian institutions. Liberals sometimes reject the bible for science, creationists seemingly repudiate science for the bible, but mainstream Christians accept information obtained both from the bible and from scientific investigations in nature. These Christians contend that both the bible and the scientific study of nature are sources of information about the origins of the earth and the universe, of life and of man.

However, though mainstream churches possess the correct doctrine, generally they've been remiss about formulating basic affirmations of that doctrine in ways which might commend themselves to a scientifically educated public. l.angdom Gilkey elaborates:

> One of theology's major tasks in the last two centuries has been to understand reflectively how religious faith ... can be reinterpreted in the light of modern science. Yet, a satisfactory (i.e., intelligible) understanding of the relationship between religion and science has not permeated American church life (or, I might add, all of American society).[11]

America's mainstream religious institutions have generally failed to organize scientific data and religious truth into a rational and understandable system, into a well-developed philosophy of science and religion available for consideration by the public. In America's bookstores there is a disheartening scarcity of accurate literature on the subject of the relationship between religion and science.

I discovered that firsthand in my own investigation for answers on the subject. Visiting every religious bookstore and library I was familiar with in my area, I found an abundance of creationist literature but a meager amount of good literature explaining the relationship between science and the bible. That was very discouraging. Consequently, it is my belief that although some people may search diligently for knowledge on the subject, most are probably rebuffed by the scant information which is both available and readable. Hence, numbers of unbelievers are tripped up by the failure of mainstream Christians to provide basic information needed for faith.

Non-Christians need to know that Christianity and science offer complementary answers to different questions. Science tells us what happens in nature and how it happens. Christianity reveals who is responsible for the natural universe and why it exists in the sense of the ultimate purpose of creation. Both are ways in which God reveals himself.

Robert Dean writes that "Science legitimately examines the observable data of the universe and seeks to unlock the secrets of how the universe is put together and how it functions." In contrast, the first two chapters of Genesis were not meant to be a scientific handbook on the universe: "Rather, these chapters affirm God as Creator and point toward his purpose in creating. The rest of the bible elaborates on that purpose."[12]

But does the theory of evolution contradict the belief that God is the Creator of the universe? Michael Green asserts that evolution does not rule out the possibility of a Creator: "Far from it. The theory of evolution sets out to explain how varied forms of life have developed from more simple forms over millions of years. Belief in a Creator sets out to explain the great Mind behind all matter. There is no contradiction between the two."[13] The theory of evolution, directed toward an explanation of how life began, does not necessarily presuppose the absence of a Creator.

Of course, all scientific theories are open to refutation, and it is quite possible that evolutionary theory might one day be abandoned. But Christians do not have to stake their faith on that possibility. Many of God's people believe that evolution is simply a process the Lord may have used to create living creatures. David Field and Peter Toon write that the Genesis account is not to be understood as "scientific:"

> Those who accept the theory of evolution and also believe the bible to be true, see the early chapters of Genesis as teaching fundamental truths about God and his relationship to the world in a form which would've been just as meaningfol for people living in the time of Moses as it is for us today. These chapters contain principles which are always true about God and his relationship to our world. The form in which the truths are expressed can be recognizied as an ancient type of literature not intended to be "scientific."[14]

But doesn't the bible teach that Adam and Eve were the first parents of all mankind, and doesn't that idea conflict with scientific theories about the origin of man? Although some scientists claim the human race descended from prehistoric ape-men who lived on earth millions of years ago, a more recent theory suggests that "we're all descended from one African 'Eve' who lived some 200,000 years ago."[15] A National Geographic article reports that molecular biologists working at the University of California, Berkeley, have discovered startling new evidence suggesting a common African origin for all mankind:

They collected tissue specimens from the placentas of 147 women of different racial backgrounds. They concentrated their analysis on the DNA, or genetic code, of a part of the human cell called the mitochondrion, which is inherited only from the mother. It had proved useful in tracing family trees. Comparing the genetic material they found that it divided into two main groups, one of which consisted exclusively of African samples. That group contained the most variations, and the researchers concluded that it therefore represented the most ancient branch of the family tree. They deduced an African "Eve," the ancestor of every living person, who lived some 200,000 years ago. Her descendants they theorized. carried her DNA to the rest of the world.[16]

These biologist say that all living people have a common ancestor from Africa who lived within the past 200,000 years. According to that theory, the human race is not descended from prehistoric ape-men. Thus scientific study does not preclude the possibility that God made the first man and woman by a special creative act and that from these two the whole human race descended.

Does the bible conflict with science? Although each source of knowledge provides information that the other does not, where the two sources overlap they basically reinforce rather than contradict each.other. First, only the bible addresses the who and why questions. The bible repeatedly indicates that "God created the heavens and the earth" (Gen. 1:1) and that He created human beings in His own image for the purpose of living in a personal relationship with Him and with each other. Second, both the bible and the scientific study of nature provide some information concerning the how questions of origins and are not contradictory when considered on the basis of valid interpretations both of scientific data and of the bible.

Of course, some ambiguities now exist between our understanding of scientific truth and our understanding of biblical truth, but as we gain more facts these conflicts will diminish. Jack Wood Sears observes, "If ultimate truth is ever attained in science and in our understanding of the bible, I believe the conflicts will evaporate completely."[17]

The facts of nature and the biblical revelation must agree because both are ways in which God reveals himself. Therefore, as Davis Young points out, "The facts of the bible and the facts of nature, . . . do not disagree but form one comprehensive, unified expression of the character and will of our Creator and Redeemer. Nature and scripture form a unity, for God is one."[18]

# 7

# WAS JESUS REALLY GOD?

O ver the ages many people have suggested various answers to the question, "Was Jesus Really God?" To some Jesus was a great prophet, to others a fine teacher, and to still others simply a moral man whose exemplary life was worthy to be imitated. Another group states that he was the Son of God. Who is right? The question of the deity of Jesus presents a sincere obstacle for many men and women.

Among the religious leaders of history, Jesus Christ is unique in the fact that he alone claimed to be God in human flesh. Josh McDowell points out, "Buddha did not claim to be God; Moses never said that he was Yahweh; Mohammed did not identify himself as Allah; and nowhere will you find Zoroaster claiming to be Ahura Mazda. Yet Jesus . . . said that he who has seen Him (Jesus) has seen the Father (John 14:9)."[1] Jesus identified himself as far more than a great prophet or teacher; he claimed to be deity, to be God.

During his time here on earth, Jesus made some fantastic claims about himself. He claimed to be the eternal God, the Creator of the universe, and mankind's only Savior.[2] Of course, anyone can *claim* to be God. The real question is whether the Lord's claim is valid: was Jesus really God?

Before I became a Christian, I often wondered about the question of the deity of Jesus. Although I realized that there had never been a man like Jesus, I wondered if he was only a great man and nothing more. Reading the works of C. S. Lewis, I was able to see the fallacy of such reasoning. In claiming deity, Jesus closed the door to any suggestion that he was just a great leader, teacher, or prophet. As C. S. Lewis stresses, Jesus never intended that alternative be open to us:

> I am trying here to prevent anyone saying the really foolish thing that people often say about Him: "I'm ready to accept Jesus as a great moral teacher, but I don't accept His claim to be God." That is the one thing we must not say. A man who was merely a man and said the sort of things Jesus said would not be a great moral teacher. He would either be a lunatic, on a level with the man who says he is a poached egg, or else he would be the Devil of Hell. You must make your choice. Either this man was, and is, the Son of God: or else a madman or something worse .... But let us not come with any patronizing nonsense about His being a great human teacher. He has not left that open to us. He did not intend to.[3]

In facing the claims of Christ, we discover there are only three alternatives, referred to as "the trilemma." Jesus was either a lunatic, a liar, or he was, and is, the Son of God. The truth of Christianity stands or falls with the validity of the tremendous claims of its Founder. If Jesus was not divine in a sense in which no other religious leader has ever claimed divinity, if he was deceived, mad, or mistaken about himself, then nothing of the most universal of religions, Christianity, would remain.

What of Christ's claim to be God—is that sheer megalomania? Was Jesus a lunatic, a sincere, but self-deluded person who is to be compared with a man who calls himself a poached egg? If Jesus was a deranged man, how could he possibly be a great moral leader or teacher? If his claims are untrue, he is much less than great.

There are places for people who go about claiming to be personages such as Napoleon, Washington, or God. A self-deceived person of that sort would probably be institutionalized to prevent him from hurting someone. Yet, in Jesus, we find no evidence of imbalance associated with a deranged person. If his claims to deity were the result of insanity, symptoms would have shown up in other areas of his life as well. But the Lord displayed no evidence of imbalance in any area. In fact, he showed his greatest composure under pressure. At his unjust trial before Pilate, Jesus maintained the highest level of balance and composure.

As C. S. Lewis maintains, "The discrepancy between the depth and sanity and (let me add) *shrewdness* of His moral teaching and the rampant megalomania which must lie behind His theological teaching unless He is indeed God, has never been satisfactorily got over."[4]

Another possibility is that Christ lied when he said he was God. Perhaps he claimed he was God simply to give weight to his teachings? Again, if Jesus was a liar, he disqualified himself from being a good teacher or a fine prophet. Josh McDowell writes, "Many will say that Jesus was a good moral teacher. Let's be realistic. How could he be a great moral teacher and knowingly mislead people at the most important point of his teaching, his own identity?"[5]

Likewise, fine prophets don't make a practice of lying, especially about being God. There is a test to discover whether someone really is a prophet: is what he says true? If not, he certainly is no prophet.

It is inconceivable for Jesus to be a liar. This view of the Savior doesn't coincide with what we know of his life and teachings. Historian Philip Schaff (1819-1893) notes:

> How, in the name of logic, common sense, and experience, could an impostor, that is a deceitful, selfish, depraved man, have invented, and consistently maintained from beginning to end, the purest and noblest character known in history with the most perfect air of truth and reality? How could he have conceived and successfully carried out a plan of unparalleled beneficence, moral magnitude, and sublimity, and sacrificed his own life for it, in the face of the strongest prejudices of his people and age.[6]

Christ's moral attributes coincide with his claims. No mere man could adopt the stance of moral purity and maintain it over the course of a lifetime. Such a man would soon betray himself by exposing some imperfection or flaw.

If Christ were just a man, those closest to him should have found some human fault. Familiarity in all our normal human relationships will eventually reveal our weaknesses and blemishes. As pointed out by John R W. Stott, that was not the case, however, with Jesus in his relationship with his disciples: "They lived in close contact with Jesus for about three years. They ate and slept together. The disciples got on one another's nerves. They quarreled. But they never found in Jesus the sins they found in themselves. Familiarity normally breeds contempt, but not in this case."[7]

These close friends of the Lord, who had been with him throughout his public ministry, did not find one hidden fault in his character.

Peter's verdict on Jesus was that He committed "no sin" (1 Peter 2:22). John's conclusion was similar: "In Him there is no sin" (1 John 3:5). The followers of Jesus emphatically agreed that he lived a sinless life. Furthermore, Christ was able to challenge even his enemies with the question: "Which one of you convicts Me of sin?" (John 8:46). No one dared to respond! Christ's moral purity was too magnificent and glorious for even his enemies to deny.

Christ could not have been either a lunatic or a liar because those viewpoints do not coincide with what we know of the depth and sanity of his life and teachings. The only other reasonable conclusion is that Jesus is exactly who he said he was—the Son of God.

What credentials did Christ provide to authenticate his claim to deity? Christ's power to heal sickness and to forgive sin emphasizes his identity. One day the Lord was preaching in a private home in Capernaum, packed solid with people eager to hear his message. Friends of a paralytic brought the man to see Christ but were unable to get in the door because of the throng of people inside. Consequently, they went up on the flat roof to let the paralytic man down with ropes to the feet of the Savior. In Mark 2:5-7 the story continues:

> And Jesus seeing their faith said to the paralytic, 'My son, your sins are forgiven.' But there were some of the scribes sitting there and reasoning in their hearts, 'Why does this man speak that way? He is blaspheming; who can forgive sins but God alone?'"

The scribes, experts in the study of the law of Moses, were knowledgeable of Jewish law and familiar with the passage in Isaiah 43 concerning forgiveness of sins. Maintaining that only God possessed authority to forgive a man's sins, the scribes reasoned,

"Why does this man speak that way? He is blaspheming: who can forgive sins but God alone."

Knowing their thoughts, Jesus quickly answered, "But in order that you may know that the Son of Man has authority on earth to forgive sins"—He said to the paralytic—'I say to you, rise, take up your pallet and go home" (Mark 2:10-11).

Christ certified that he had the power to forgive the man's sins. How did he do this? He confirmed the invisible transaction (forgiving the man's sins) by a visible act (healing the man's physical infirmity). Christ responded with action the people could see. He healed the man's illness that people might know he had authority to deal with the man's sins. Lewis Sperry Chafer notes:

> None on earth has authority or right to forgive sin. None could forgive sin save the One against whom all have sinned. When Christ forgave sin, as He certainly did, He was not exercising a human perogative. Since none but God can forgive sin, it is conclusively demonstrated that Christ, since He forgave sins, is God.[8]

Every miracle that Jesus the Savior worked during his earthly ministry was designed to prove to man that he is God. When John the Baptist sent two men to inquire about Christ's divinity, Jesus said to them, "Go and report to John what you hear and see: the blind rcceive sight and the lame walk, the lepers are cleansed and the deaf hear, and the dead are raised up, and the poor have the gospel preached to them" (Matt. 11:4-5).

Christ demonstrated a power over natural forces which could only belong to God: he turned water into wine (John 2:3-10); stilled a raging storm (Mark 4:37-41); and fed 5,000 people from five loaves and two fish (Matt. 14:15-21). He did these and other miracles as proofs of his divinity.

The words of Christ are another line of proof which establish his deity. Wherever Jesus traveled, crowds of people followed and listened intently to his message. Common folks recognized that there was something different about this teacher and marveled at the authority of Jesus' words. Christ's teaching manner was radically different from the method of the religious scribes and rabbis. The rabbis were revered persons in the land, admired for their meticulous observance of the law, but here was One who spoke with greater authority than they.

The procedure of those earthly teachers consisted in referring to the thoughts and teachings of others; they quoted first one great teacher and then another. In contrast, the teaching of Jesus was highly original. Instead of frequently quoting other teachers, the Lord offered his own insight into religious affairs: "And everyone who hears *these words of Mine*, and does not act upon them, will be like a foolish man" (Matt. 7:26).

The people had never heard teaching like this before: "When Jesus had finished these words, the multitudes were amazed at His teaching; for He was teaching them as one having authority, and not as their scribes" (Matt. 7:28-29). These men and women recognized the difference. Scribes taught them from authorities; Christ taught them with authority.

Christ's ultimate credential confirming his claim to deity was his resurrection from the dead. The resurrection of Jesus is the foundation stone for all that Christians believe and experience. The apostle Paul noted: "If Christ has not been raised, then our preaching is vain, your faith also is vain" (1 Cor. 15:14). Without the resurrection of Jesus, our faith would have no objective validity.

Did the resurrection of Jesus Christ actually happen? Does this unusual event have a historically acceptable basis? In considering such questions, some people wonder why the death of Jesus should have significance as opposed to history's countless other executions and martyrdoms. Others have died unjustly and inspired those who came after them. In a similar way, couldn't Christ's death simply have inspired his followers to carry on his cause?

The significance of the death of Christ as opposed to others is readily apparent. Jesus did not die in the service of a cause, as we normally use the word; he was not a leader whose death inspired his followers to further devotion toward the achievement of a common goal. On the "before" side of the resurrection, Christ's death had none of the effects we associate with an inspiring death. His disciples were not inspired into a revolutionary or retributive rage; they were utterly disillusioned by his death. During the days immediately following the Lord's death, they were a sorry, frightened group of men.

Suddenly they changed! In spite of their former doubts, these same disciples were out on the streets of Jerusalem fearlessly proclaiming the name of Jesus. What caused this sudden dramatic change? Only the bodily resurrection of Jesus could have caused the profound transformation of the disciples.

The disciples proclaimed the resurrection as sober historical fact.[9] Their claim was based not on speculation but on empirical truth. They observed the risen Christ, talked with him, and ate with him. The resurrection event was a public spectacle and a matter of public record. It was not done in a corner. That the Bible presents history on this matter is a fact beyond serious dispute.

Lord Darling, former Chief Justice of England, examining the evidence from a judicial point of view, writes, "There exists such overwhelming evidence, positive and negative, factual and circumstantial, that no intelligent jury in the world could fail to bring in a verdict that the resurrection story is true."[10]

There is only one explanation that adequately fits the facts: Jesus Christ rose from death. If Jesus has risen, he is still alive and capable of entering the lives of those who invite him. Because Jesus is really "there," we can experience and know him today.

Was Jesus really God? Everything about Jesus points to the fact that he was not just a mere man, but God: the life Jesus lived, the works he performed, the words he spoke, his death and resurrection. All stress the fact that he is God!

# 8

# WHY DOES GOD ALLOW EVIL & SUFFERING?

One of the most pressing problems of our time is the poignant question of why innocent people suffer: why are babies born deformed or retarded; why are there wars where blameless adults and children are maimed or killed; why are there handicaps and diseases, natural disasters and tragic accidents, rapes and murders. Why does God allow evil and suffering to exist? Is He somehow powerless to prevent it all happening? If God is all-loving and all-powerful, why did he make a world with so much misery and pain?[1]

The problem of evil and suffering, perhaps the most obstinate barrier to belief in God, creates a genuine difficulty for many people concerning Christiany. As Elton Trueblood notes, "So far as rational faith is concerned the problem of evil is our most serious contemporary problem."[2]

Throughout history folks have wrestled with the classical problem of why an all-good and all-powerful God would allow evil to exist. C. S. Lewis voiced our apparent dilemma: "If God were good, He would wish to make His creatures perfectly happy, and if God were almighty, He would be able to do what He wished. But the creatures are not happy. Therefore God lacks either goodness, or power, or both."[3] In other words, either God does not care, or he is powerless to prevent the tragedies and sufferings in our world.

Is it possible to believe in a good, all-powerful God while living in a world shattered by suffering? Many sincere seekers would like to believe in a loving, omnipotent God but wonder whether such faith is reasonable. Do Christians have any valid reasons for believing in a God of power and of love? Christians have solid grounds for believing that a God of goodness and power has reasons for allowing evil and suffering. Although the Bible, the source of our knowledge of God's character, does not present a complete and systematic explanation of the reasons for suffering, it does give some important clues.

First, the Bible teaches that God is all-powerful: "Behold, I am the Lord, the God of all flesh; is anything too difficult for Me?" (Jer. 32:27). God is certainly powerful enough to deal with evil. He has demonstrated over and over that he has the capability to end evil and injustice. Thus it is a grave mistake for us to question God's omnipotence. God *could* overpower the world. By wiping out men like Hitler and Mussolini and Hussein and Putin, God could stop wars. Our Creator could "zap" the vehicles of all careless drivers to prevent such people from driving. God could take excess wealth from the rich and redistribute it to the world's poverty stricken masses.

But God has chosen not to intervene. Why? Is it because he is powerless to stop such events as wars, accidents, and poverty? No! Free will is the reason an all-powerful God does not hasten to remedy every situation. God's main purpose in creating men and women was to allow them to enjoy his love and to give them an opportunity to return it. But love is voluntary; it cannot be forced. Consequently, God provided mankind with what is usually called a free will. Of course, God could have made people like mechanical robots or puppets dancing on strings. But he wanted people who would really love him and obey him, of their own free choice. C. S. Lewis goes on to point out that if God exercised his power to stop every tragedy, men would no longer be souls with free agency:

> We can, perhaps, conceive of a world in which God corrected the results of this abuse of free will by His creatures at every moment: so that a wooden beam became soft as grass when it was used as a weapon, and the air refused to obey me if I attempted to set up in it the sound waves that carry lies or insults. But such a world would be one in which wrong actions were impossible, and in which, therefore, freedom of will would be void . . . . That God can and does, on occasions, modify the behavior of matter and produce what we call miracles, is part of the Christian faith; but the very conception of a common, and therefore, stable, world, demands that these occasions should be extremely rare![4]

In the process of giving us freedom of choice, God has chosen to limit his own power in certain ways. For instance, when God made man free, he thereby imposed a limit on what he would do in dealing with mankind. Freedom is a great blessing, but it is also fraught with great peril. While God allows men and women to make their own choices, he also allows them to reap the consequences of those choices. This is the clue to the moral evil in the world and the explanation for much of the pain and suffering that results from human sin.

A great deal of the suffering in the world is caused by human wrong-doing, by "moral evil." Thefts, murders, rapes, wars and so on are all traceable to our wrong decisions. However, many of our other problems are not of our own making. "Natural evil" is found in the effects on people of distortion in the natural environment. Earthquakes, hurricanes, volcanoes, floods, many diseases, and other calamities can bring untold suffering to human beings. How do we explain the natural disasters that wrack havoc on mankind?

There is also a sense in which God has given a certain freedom to the universe itself. Rohen Dean writes that another way in which God has limited himself is by:

> ... placing us in a universe in which certain orderly processes are at work. This does not mean that ours is a universe that runs by ironclad, unchangeable rules. God is no celestial Clockmaker who has made the universe, wound it up, and now has left it to tick away according to its own mechanism. This is God's universe; he knows and cares; he sometimes moves in ways that seem miraculous by those who assume that natural laws are fixed and rigid. On the other hand, God is not constantly intervening to change certain ordered processes of nature.[5]

God has set up certain natural laws and systems to govern the universe. For example, the law of gravity keeps us from floating off into space. But the same law will cause pain to someone who jumps from the top of a tall building. Of course, God *could* catch such a person. There have been times when God has done miraculous things to save lives; sometimes God makes exceptions to the laws of nature. But the majority of the time God lets nature take its course. Natural disasters are not intended to cause suffering:

> Consider the hurricane, the earths way of releasing pentup heat and energy. The hurricane is not meant to cause suffering, but if people ignore the warnings of nature, they will be injured by hurricanes. The same is true of faultlines,

such as the San Andreas Fault. Faultlines are necessary to keep the earth from just breaking apart. But if people insist upon building houses on the San Andreas fault, as they do, then they are going to suffer when an earthquake comes. Such suffering does not result from God's intentions, but comes rather from man's foolishness. We can either go along with natural forces and accommodate ourselves to them, or we can ignore them and be hurt by them.[6]

God opted to create men and women with free will, to allow us to experience both the love and the joy, the pain and the suffering of our existence. Would we have it otherwise? God could have made mankind with a predetermined destiny, but then we would have been nothing more than mere robots. Only through the mechanism of free choice could humanity attain any significance or real worth.

Second, the Word of God teaches that our Maker is a God of love who cares deeply for mankind: "'Indeed, the Lord will give what is good" (Ps. 85:12). Scripture emphasizes that God always has the best interest of humanity in mind in all his decisions. In considering the question of divine goodness, is it God's highest purpose for humans that we live a completely pain-free existence? Would a good God want to prevent all suffering and pain?

C. S. Lewis comments that when we think of God's goodness, what we really want is "a grandfather in heaven, a senile benevolence who as they say, 'liked to see young people enjoying themselves,' and whose plan for the universe was simply that it might be truly said at the end of each day, 'a good time was had by all'"[7]

Such a concept of the goodness of God is based on the faulty assumption that a fun-filled, pain-free life equals happiness. However, genuine, deep-seated happiness is something much more profound than the fleeting enjoyment of the moment. Actually fun and happiness have little in common. Fun is the emotion we experience *during* an act. Happiness is the deeper, more abiding emotion we feel *after* an act.

Of course, there is nothing wrong with enjoying fun activities. Going to a movie or an amusement park, observing or participating in a sport, engaging in a hobby or a game, are fun activities that help us rest and relax. But these forms of fun do not contribute in any lasting way to our happiness, because their positive effects end when the fun ends. John Allan notes that the difficulties of life often bring us more lasting happiness:

> Sometimes pain, stress, and struggle are actually necessary experiences if life is to be all it should be. It is often in trying times that we learn the most important lessons and gain touch with our feelings at the very deepest level. Looking back on my life so far, I can think of a lot of fun times; they were enjoyable, of course, and I wouldn't have missed them for anything. but they didnt honestly benefit me much. The deepest and most precious experiences of my life are all associated with times of difficulty and pressure.[8]

True happiness is not precluded by suffering. There is a certain amount of pain involved whenever people are moving to a higher level of growth; often we learn some of life's most important lessons in the school of suffering. Lewis Drummond stresses that we should "see our suffering selves not just as victims but as students, students growing into maturity. The object of life is not ease but the maturity of the human soul."[9]

Many people have had to suffer in order to turn to God. Until they lost their material wealth or their health or someone dear to them, they had no desire for spiritual matters. C. S. Lewis says,

"God whispers to us in our pleasures, speaks in our conscience, but shouts in our pains; it is His megaphone to rouse a deaf world."[10]

In my own life, I realize that God "shouted" to me, "called" me, through my daughter Karen's death. In Billy Graham's book, *Facing Death and the Lift After*, there is a beautiful chapter entitled, "Why Do Some Die So Soon?" Referring to what C. S. Lewis said about God shouting in our pains, Graham notes:

> No one likes to be shouted at, and yet God loves us so much that when troubles come, He is there to call us closer to Him. Children may be the little trumpet players who bring us to our senses, and to our knees. Jesus said, 'Let the little children come to me, and do not hinder them, for the kingdom of heaven belongs to such as these'" (Matthew 19:14 NIV).[11]

Reading the passage, I understood that God used pain and tragedy to compel me to make a search for truth, however arduous that search would be. Hence, God brought good out of my suffering.

Although various kinds of suffering in life are inevitable, we must realize it is our reaction to suffering, not the suffering itself, that determines whether the experience is one of blessing or blight. We can allow suffering to drive us to Christ, or we can allow suffering drive us to bitterness and despair.

Is our "happiness" the chief purpose of God's creation? Is the best of all possible worlds one in which human pleasure and painlessness prevail? We must answer, "No!" For God to shield us from all suffering and pain would be to rob us of a greater good, to rob us of discovering the heart of God.

In thinking about pain and suffering, whether it be physical or mental, we must remember that we are not alone. God not only is aware of our sorrow and pain, but also suffers with us and for us. The bible emphasizes the sufferings of the Lord Jesus Christ: "He was despised and forsaken of men, a man of sorrows, and acquainted with grief" (Isa. 53:3).

Scripture says that Christ identifies with our suffering: "For since He Himself was tempted in that which He has suffered, He is able to come to the aid of those who are tempted" (Heb. 2:18). "For we do not have a high priest who cannot sympathize with our weaknesses, but one who has been tempted in all things as we are, yet without sin" (Heb. 4:15). God not only loves us and hears our cries for help, he comes to us as a fellow sufferer. David Field and Peter Toon write:

> God himself did not remain aloof from suffering, but in the person of Jesus of Nazareth entered the world and endured pain of mind and body on our behalf. Even though the world has gone wrong, God has taken responsibility for it. Jesus died for that very sin and evil which has caused the pain and distortion of creation. He died the death due to us, and when we suffer he enters into close identity with us, as some one who has gone through it all himself. Above all, his death was "for the sins of the whole world": He made it possible for there to be a new start, a whole new creation. His rising from death was the beginning of this, its fulfillment is still to come.[12]

Christians can respond to pain and suffering with faith and hope because of the redemptive power of the death and resurrection of Jesus Christ. We know that pain and death do not have the last word, for beyond suffering and death are life and resurrection. Ultimately, when Jesus comes back again, all pain, suffering, sickness, and death will be destroyed forever. "And He shall wipe away every tear from their eyes; and there shall no longer be any death; there shall no longer be any mourning, or crying, or pain; the first things have passed away" (Rev. 21:4). Eventually God will transform this chaotic, unjust world into an orderly, just domain where we will enjoy everlasting life in a perfect realm.

In the meantime Jesus commands us to be agents of compassion and justice in a decaying world. We know that suffering can be redeemed and that we can be used of God to bring this redemption to bear. Hence, as Cliffe Knechtle notes, Christians should "use science, medicine, law, business, education, and any other tool to alleviate suffering, prolong life, promote justice, and enhance the quality of life."[13]

Why does God allow evil and suffering? Although we only see a few threads in the tapestry of life and God's will, we are not left to guess about God's character. Paul Little notes:

> Life is like a fabric with many edges which are blurred, many events and circumstances we do not understand. But they are to be interpreted by the clarity we see in the center, the cross of Christ. We are not left to guess about the goodness of God from isolated bits of data. He has clearly revealed His character and dramatically demonstrated it to us in the Cross. 'He that spared not His own Son, but delivered Him up for us all, how shall He not with Him also freely give us all things?'" (Rom. 8:32).[14]

# 9

# IS THE BIBLE TRULY GOD'S WORD?

The question of the authenticity of the Bible produces a serious hindrance to faith for some folks. These men and women wonder whether the bible is a trustworthy source of information, a genuine revelation from God. Before my conversion, I often wondered about the question myself. Non-Christian religions also have sacred books which claim to be God's revelation. How could I know for sure that the bible alone is truly God's Word?

A variety of objective evidence validates the bible's authority as the true Word of God. Some data on which judgment about the bible can be based includes its unity, its divine inspiration, its fulfilled prophecy, its historical accuracy, and its miracles.

One indication that the bible is God's Word is its unity. Although the book was composed by men, its unity flows from its source in God. The Scriprures were written over a period of fifteen hundred years by about forty different authors displaying such widely varied backgrounds as the following:

Moses was a well-educated leader; Joshua was a military general; Solomon was a king; Daniel was a prime minister; Amos was a herdsman; Nehemiah was a cupbearer; Peter was a fisherman; Luke was a doctor; Matthew was a tax collector; Paul was a rabbi. These authors wrote in different places: Moses in the wilderness; Paul inside prison walls; Jeremiah in a dungeon; Luke while traveling; John on the isle of Patmos. The biblical writings were composed on three different continents, Asia, Africa, and Europe, and in three different languages, Hebrew, Aramaic, and Greek.

Considering the diverse factors, we would expect the bible to be a confused and disjointed text, anything but harmonious. Yet the bible displays unity. From beginning to end it relates one unfolding story of God's plan of salvation for mankind through the person of Jesus Christ. Jesus is the theme of the entire bible. Josh McDowell and Don Stewart write:

> The Old Testament is the preparation (Isaiah 40:3). The Gospels are the manifestation (John 1:29). The Book of Acts is the propagation {Acts 1:8). The Epistles give the explanation (Colossians 1:27). The Book of Revelation is the consummation (Revelation 1:7). The bible is all about Jesus.[1]

The unity of scripture is a significant clue the bible's origin is divine. It is highly unlikely that the authors wrote the bible on their own. The writers were highly diverse people, separated from each other by hundreds of years and hundreds of miles. Nevertheless, there is a unity which binds the whole together, a complete accord. The only reasonable way the sixty-six books of the bible could have come together with such complete harmony and continuity is that the ultimate author was God himself.

Another reason we know the bible is God's Word is because of evidence of its divine inspiration. The bible is by far the number one bestseller of all history with untold millions of people considering it to be the greatest book ever published.

No other book can equal its poetic beauty or profound wisdom. The Holy Bible claims, however, to be more than just the world's greatest book. It claims to be written by divine inspiration, to be the true Word of God.

Yet there are those who contend that the bible is only inspired in a way similar to that of all great literature. People holding the viewpoint of natural inspiration acknowledge the bible has high ethics, morals, and insights but say the bible is only an achievement on the same level as other great writings. The viewpoint denies there is a supernatural dimension to the writing of scripture and claims the composers of the bible were no more inspired than were authors such as Shakespeare, Milton, or Confucius.

The natural inspiration view is obviously inadequate. The bible clearly claims to be more than merely inspiring literature. Two significant bible verses speak to the heart of the matter. One notes that "All scripture is inspired by God" (2 Tim. 3:16). Another verse states, "For no prophecy was ever made by an act of human will, but men moved by the Holy Spirit spoke from God" (2 Peter 1:21). As Paul Little notes:

> The Holy Bible originated in the mind of God, not in the mind of man. It was given man by inspiration. It is important to understand this term because its biblical meaning is different from that which we often give it in everyday language. The bible is not inspired as the writings of a great novelist are inspired, or as Bach's music was inspired. Inspiration, in the biblical sense, means that God so superintended the writers of Scripture that they wrote what He wanted them to write and were kept from error in so doing.[2]

Although the writers of Scripture were moved by God to record that which he desired, they were not robots through whom he merely dictated. Rather, God worked in a supernatural way, using each individual writer's mind, personality, and experiences to convey his divine message to mankind. Thus God, by his Spirit, guaranteed the reliability of the very words that were written without depriving the writers of their individuality.

The bible is clear that its origin is divine, that it is not merely inspiring literature. Don Stewart observes, "The biblical doctrine of inspiration means that the bible is God's accurate revelation of himself. Thus, the bible cannot be categorized with other literature that causes the human heart to be challenged. It is inspired, not merely inspiring. It is the Word of God."[3]

A third way we can see the bible is God's Word is the remarkable number of fulfilled prophecies it contains. In the Bible there are literally hundreds of prophecies foretelling persons, places, and events hundreds of years before their occurrence. Only God, who is outside our time space existence and our finite knowledge, could foretell events in history with such absolute accuracy before they happen.

Prophecies of the bible were not based on vague generalities. Modern fortunetellers give predictions such as: "Soon a handsome man will enter your life." In contrast, bible prophecies were specific in detail, full of contingencies which couldn't be rigged in advance in an attempt to produce fulfillment. One of the best resources detailing the importance of biblical prophecy is J. Barton Payne's *Encyclopedia of Biblical Prophecy* (Harper and Row, 1973). This book contains 754 pages with 1,817 entries covering all the biblical predictions in both the Old and New Testaments, as well as a complete discussion of all 8,352 predictive verses in the bible.

It is impossible for biblical prophecies to be of human or accidental origin. It is well known that forecasting a single event with only one detail affords a fifty percent probability of fulfillment by the law of chance. If an additional detail is added, the chances of successful prediction fall to twenty-five percent. Adding a third leaves only one chance in eight of a fulfilled prophecy. In the bible there are over three hundred predicted details of Christ's first coming. Left to chance, there would be virtually no way predictions of this nature could have been fulfilled.

In addition, the prophecies of scripture could not have been written after events and pawned off as prophecies, because in many instances the fulfillment of prophecy did not take place until hundreds of years after the prophet's death. In some cases the fulfillment came after the completion of the Old Testament and even its translation into Greek.

What are some of the incredibly specific prophecies of the Bible? Besides the scores of predictions concerning what would happen to certain cities, nations, and people, there are several hundred prophecies pointing to the coming of the Messiah that were perfectly fulfilled in Jesus Christ. David Dewitt lists some of those predictions:

> The place of his birth (Micah 5:2 and Matthew 2:1), that He was to be born of one called a virgin (Isaiah 7:14 and Matthew 1:23), His lift-style as a suffering servant (Isaiah 53), His triumphal entry into Jerusalem on a colt of a donkey (Zechariah 9:9 and Matthew 21:4-11), the betrayal for thirty pieces of silver (Zechariah 11:12 and Matthew 26:15), His humble attitude at His trial (Isaiah 53:7 and Matthew 27:11-14), the piercing of His hands and His feet (Psalm 22:16 and Matthew 27:35), His being beaten and spit upon (Isaiah 50:6 and Matthew 26:67), the gall and vinegar they gave Him to drink while on the cross (Psalm 69:21 and Matthew 27:34), the casting of lots for His clothing at the crucifixion (Psalm

22:18 and Matthew 27:35), the burial (Isaiah 53:9 and John 20:28), and that He was to be called God (Isaiah 9:6 and John 4:25-26).[4]

The odds that one person could fulfill these Messianic prophecies by chance are astronomical, but Jesus of Nazareth fulfilled these and many more. The prophetic character of Scripture stands alone in its content, completeness, and accuracy; it underscores the fact that the bible is the true Word of God.

An additional way we can know the bible is God's Word is through its historical accuracy. The importance of the biblical story lies in its being real, historical fact. It is because certain events really happened that the Christian has grounds for belief. Therefore, the historical accuracy of the bible is of vital importance to us. Is the bible grounded and rooted in history? Historians generally apply three tests to any piece of literature of history to determine if it is accurate or reliable: the bibliographical test, the internal evidence test, and the external evidence test. In the interest of brevity, only the historicity of the New Testament will be examined here.[5]

First, using the bibliographical test, an examination of the textual transmission by which documents reach us, historians have determined that the text of the New Testament is reliable. It has more manuscript authority than any piece of literature from antiquity. John Warwick Montgomery observes, "To be skeptical of the resultant text of the New Testament books is to allow all of classical antiquity to slip into obscurity, for no documents of the ancient period are as well attested bibliographically as the New Testament."[6] Fenton Hort adds that 'In the variety and fullness of the evidence on which it rests the text of the New Testament stands absolutely and unapproachably alone among ancient prose writings."[7] According to the bibliographical test, the New Testament is accurate, reliable history.

The bibliographical test ascertains only that the text we now have is what was originally recorded. The internal evidence test determines whether that written record is credible and to what extent. Again, historians have established that the New Testament account is credible history.

The New Testament writers were eyewimesses to the historical Jesus and his mighty works. Peter says, "For we did not follow cleverly devised tales when we made known to you the power and coming of our Lord Jesus Christ, but we were eyewitnesses of His majesty" (2 Peter 1:16). The writers of the New Testament gave firsthand testimony.

But, given the fact that the documents are an authentic apostolic witness, are they an honest acoount? Can we believe what the apostles said? We can believe the apostles because not only did they claim personal knowledge of the facts, but they also appealed to the firsthand knowledge of critics and other contemporaries concerning evidence about Jesus.

Don Stewart observes, "It must be remembered that not all of the eyewitnesses to the biblical miracles were believers. If the disciples tended to distort the facts, the unbelieving eyewitnesses would have immediatdy objected."[8] The best possible jury to test what the gospel writers said was their own contemporaries. If the writers had been contradicted by the facts, the people would have quickly repudiated their testimony. Yet their record went unchallenged.

The third test of historicity is that of external evidence. Historians seek to find other sources which substantiate the literature under question.[9] Once more, the New Testament stands as the world's most documented ancient literature. Barry Wood writes:

> There exists today a vast amount of material written from the first century through the fourth century which is either knowledgeable of or quotes from the New Testament. Such men as Clement of Rome (A.D. 95), Ignatius (A.D. 70-110), Polycarp (A.D. 70-156), and Irenaeus (A.D. 180) along with many others recognize the New Testament as divine scripture written by the apostles.[10]

Combined evidence from the three tests, the bibliographical, the internal, and the external, leaves no doubt about the historical accuracy of the New Testament.

Miracles are another indication that the Bible is the Word of God. The Bible, from beginning to end, testifies that God has broken into human history and performed miraculous deeds.

But why should we believe in the biblical miracles? Aren't there many other religions that claim miracles as a basis of the truth of their faith? When the facts are considered, we discover that the miracles of the Bible are on a different level from those of other religions. Josh McDowell points out that miracles God performed were signs to testify of his existence and power or to meet a specific need:

> The miracle stories as recorded in the Bible are always for a definite purpose and never to show off. There is always a logical reason for them. For exampk, there were 5,000 people who were in immediate need of food, which was promptly provided by miraculous means (Luke 9:12-17). At a wedding feast in Cana, the wine had run out. The need for

wine was met by Jesus, who turned water into wine (John 2:1-11). The miracles of Jesus were performed out of love and compassion to those who were afflicted. They were also meant to be objective signs to the people that He was the promised Messiah, since one of the creden tials of the Messiah would be signs and miracles.[11]

Miracles serve to confirm that the bible is the Word of God. The basic purpose of miracles, to demonstrate God's involvement with mankind, extends not only to persons who directly observed the events but also to persons who subsequently read of them in God's inspired Word. Miraculous signs confirm the truth of the Word which is spoken about Christ, pointing men to him as the Son of God and the Savior of their souls: "But these [miracles of Jesus] have been written that you may believe that Jesus is the Christ, the Son of God; and that believing you may have life in His name" John 20:31).

Is the bible truly God's Word? Scriptures's unity, its divine inspiration, its fulfilled prophecy, its historical accuracy and its miracles all serve to prove that the bible alone is the true Word of God. Billy Graham writes:

The Bible easily qualifies as the only Book in which is God's revelation. There are many bibles of different religions; there is the Muslim Koran, the Buddhist Canon of Sacred Scripture, the Zoroastrian Zend-Avesta, and the Brahman Vedas. All of these have been made accessible to us by reliable translations. Anyone can read them, comparing them with the bible, and judge for themselves. It is soon discovered that all these non-Christian bibles have parts of truth in them, but they are all developments ultimately in the wrong direction. . . . Even the most casual observ er soon discovers that the bible is radically different. It is the only Book that offers man a redemption and points the way out of his dilemmas. It is our one sure guide in an unsure world.[12]

# 10

# WHAT IS GOD LIKE?

Some Christians avoid discussing subjects such as eternal punishment, because they think questions of that sort are simply smoke-screens set up by non-believers to dodge the real issues. Generally, however, when non-Christians ask that kind of question, they aren't setting up a smokescreen, but simply asking a sincere question that needs a proper response. Their real question is, "What is God like?"

Seekers like that wonder: "Would a God of love actually consign people to unending punishment?" The Bible teaches both the goodness of God and the reality of hell and trying to reconcile these two truths presents a difficult problem for many non-Christians.

On the one hand, Scripture emphasizes that "God is love" (1 John 4:8). From Genesis to Revelation, we find verses such as the following: "Just as a father has compassion on his children, so the Lord has compassion on those who fear him" (Ps. 103:13); "I have loved you with an everlasting love; therefore I have drawn you with lovingkindness" (Jer. 31:3); "For God so loved the world, that He gave His only begotten Son, that whoever believes in Him should not perish, but have eternal life" (John 3:16). Without question, the Bible teaches the love, the grace, and the goodness of God.

On the other hand, the Word of God also stresses the reality of hell. In fact, much of what the bible says about the place of eternal punishent is in Jesus' own words. Jesus used

expressions such as "unquenchable fire" (Mark 9:43), "weeping and gnashing of teeth" (Matt. 13:42), and "their worm does not die" (Mark 9:44) to teach the horrible fate of the wicked. Other New Testament writers support Christ's ideas about punishment for the wicked after death. Positively, the doctrine of hell is a basic teaching of God's Word.

So, how do we reconcile the goodness of God with eternal punishment? The two truths, God's love and God's holiness, must be balanced. Harold Bryson states that overemphasis of either truth could lead to prominent distortions of God's character:

> Stressing God's love to the neglect of his holiness presents the picture that God is a sentimental grandfather. But the bible presents God, not as a tolerating, gentle grandfather, but as a loving, kind father. Reading sentimentality into God's character misses what the bible says about God's stern judgment. On the other extreme, some have presented God as a tyrant who enjoys seeing the wicked suffer; as a stern judge, anxiously waiting to give every person what he deserves. The bible's picture of God has the correct balance. Jesus showed the Father to be one who knows, cares, and gives help to his creatures. The depth of God's love for humanity is seen when he went to the cross . . . . Jesus presented God perfectly with a balance between God's love and God's holiness that explains his severity on sin.[1]

The bible declares God to be holy, and God's holiness demands judgment and punishment for sin. But Scripture also reveals that

God is merciful and loving; he has provided a way to escape condemnation by sending his Son to die in our place. Christ came to deal with sin on the cross, to offer forgiveness to those who want to be saved. Men and women who say "yes" to that offer are voluntarily allowing God to make them citizens of his eternal kingdom. But those who say "no" to God's loving offer have made their own decision. The eternal consequences of the rebellion of each unsaved person will have been that person's choice, not God's.

But what about those who have never heard the gospel, those who die in childhood, those who are mentally retarded or mentally ill, and those who lived before Christ? Where do they stand in the eyes of God? It is quite legitimate for us to ask how God will judge these people.

First, will God condemn billions of people who have never even heard the gospel message? Some people are sincerely troubled by that question. In an article in a Baptist journal, it was estimated that "of the world's population, 1.7 billion are Christian. Another 2.1 billion have been exposed to the gospel but are not Christian, and 1.3 billion have never even heard the gospel"[2] What is the spiritual fate of this estimated 1.3 billion who have never heard?

The answer is we do not know how God will judge those who have never heard. William Spurrier writes, "Some theologians . . . assume too much knowledge about whom God 'damns' or 'saves.' The fact is we do not know and can never know in this life."[3]

However, when we think of those who never hear the gospel, we find comfort in Abraham's idea, "Shall not the Judge of all the earth deal justly" (Gen. 18:25) and in Job's observation, "Surely, God will not act wickedly, and the Almighty will not pervert justice" (Job 34:12). Although the bible doesn't develop the theme as deeply as we would like, such principles help us to trust that God will do the right thing.

Clark Pinnock concludes that there is a hard-line view on this subject which states that there is no possibility of salvation apart from an explicit faith relationship with the Jesus of the Christian proclamation, a view that would exclude the majority of the human race:

> Needless to say, this opinion has caused sensitive Christians much pain and posed an almost insuperable barrier to those who might otherwise be interested in the gospel There is another view, equally ancient and capable of validation from the Scriptures, that holds that God deals with people where he finds them. If he finds them in paganism, as he found Abraham and Melchizedek, he can communicate with them in that milieu. God has not revealed all his arrangements to us, and we are not required to speculate about the outcome of judgments God has not yet shared with us.[4]

The issue is not with those who have never heard the gospel, but with those who have heard. God does hold accountable men and women who are aware of the Christian message. The Bible is clear about the judgment which awaits people who refuse God's loving offer: "He who believes in the Son has eternal life; but he who does not obey the Son shall not see life, but the wrath of God abides on him" (John 3:36).

Second, what is the eternal destiny of those who die in childhood or who are mentally retarded or mentally ill? How can we know the young or the mentally incapacitated are safe in our Heavenly Father's arms? It is vital for us to confront these questions of the fate of the young and mentally weak.

Although the Bible is not explicit on this issue, it does provide us with some principles which suggest that children and the mentally deficient are not lost. David Dewitt observes:

> Biblical evidence indicates that people unable consciously to choose Christ are not held accountable for rejecting Him. Deuteronomy 1:39 reads, "Moreover, your little ones who you said would become a prey, and your sons, who this day have no knowledge of good or evil shall enter there, and I will give it to them, and they shall possess it." The "it" of that verse is not eternal life; "it" is the promised land of Palestine, not heaven. But the principle is the same. Those who are not able to be accountable were not held accountable.[5]

Other passages also imply that Children and the mentally afflicted are in some special way kept by the power of God. In Matt. 18:10 Jesus warns, "See that you do not despise one of these little ones, for I say to you, that their angels in heaven continually behold the face of My Father who is in heaven." In Matt. 18:14 the Lord says, "Thus it is not the will of your Father who is in heaven that one of these little ones perish." Finally, in Matt. 19:14 our Savior emphasizes, "Let the children alone, and do not hinder them from coming to Me; for the kingdom of heaven belongs to such as these."

An inference based upon what we know of God as revealed in Scripture is that little ones and the mentally deficient are under the election of grace. The specter of a young child or a mentally ill person suffering eternal punishment is entirely unacceptable in a moral universe. We could never conceive of a God whose nature is love, planning or allowing such a hideous miscarriage of justice. Therefore, we can believe that young children and the mentally ill are accepted into God's presence on the basis of Christ's atoning work even though they are incapable of exercising personal faith in him. As Barry Wood points out:

> Children are innocent until they individually respond to God in rebellion. This statement would imply that children or the mentally retarded are not accountable. Only Gods knows when a person is ready for the gospel. Some retarded persons never come to the age of accountability and are under God's watchcare, just like a little child. It is my understanding that children who die go immediately to be with the Lord, perhaps escorted by guardian angels (see Matthew 18:10) into the presence ofGod.[6]

Third, what is the spiritual fate of those who lived before Christ? How could any of them have come to a knowledge of the true God? The basis of salvation has always been the sacrificial death, burial, and resurrection of Jesus Christ. Although the saving work of Christ was future, God saw it from before the foundation of the earth. Not bound by time, the Lord applied the benefits of Christ's death to all who called upon God for salvation. As David Dewitt notes, God's plan to restore man to a relationship with Himself has never changed:

> The message of salvation in the Old Testament is the same as in the New. Man is described as a sinner separated from God (Isaiah 59:2) and in need of a redeemer (Job 19:25). The only way people could get to God was by grace (Psalm 6:2) through faith (Genesis 15:6), and not by their own works (Isaiah 64:6). The object of their faith was the personal Messiah (Isaiah 53:3) who would be God Himself (Isaiah 9:6) when He would come to earth as a baby (Isaiah 7:14). They needed to have faith in the Messiah who would come, just as we need to have faith in the Messiah who did come.[7]

The details of Christ's coming were progressively revealed.

Each age has received more details, and even we who are living today do not see as clearly as we will when Jesus returns. But the essential message of the gospel has remained unchanged since God first revealed the need of a sacrifice to Adam.

What is God like? From the bible we learn that God trusts people with the power of choice: "I have set before you life and death, the blessing and the curse. So choose life" (Deut. 30:19). God gives every person the chance to choose either right or wrong, blessing or destruction. He forces no one to go in either direction.

Some think God continues calling the lost soul and reaching out to them with his grace, even to the very last moment of the person's life. Saint Faustina wrote in Diary entry 1507:

> All grace flows from mercy, and the last hour abounds with mercy for us. Let no one doubt concerning the goodness of God; even if a person's sins were as dark as night, God's mercy is stronger than our misery. One thing alone is necessary: that the sinner set ajar the door of his heart, be it ever so little, to let in a ray of God's merciful grace, and then God will do the rest. But poor is the soul who has shut the door on God's mercy, even at the last hour. It was just such souls who plunged Jesus into deadly sorrow in the Garden of Olives; indeed, it was from His Most Merciful Heart that divine mercy flowed out.[8]

Therefore, as noted above, some feel our Savior keeps calling His lost children, clear up to the end of life:

> The Good Shepherd keeps seeking out His lost sheep, right up until they draw their last breath. Even if they are

unconcious at the end, then in the very depths of their souls He searches them out. That is why we can never be sure if some soul was truly lost or not, even if they never showed any outward sign of repentance and faith at all; the Lord searches them out in the depths of their hearts in ways we cannot see. Their "one last chance" is at the moment of death. All we can do is to entrust them to God's mercy.[9]

In regard to a last chance, scripture tells us that when Jesus was crucified, "Two other men, both criminals, were also led out with Him to be executed. When they came to the place called the Skull, they crucified him there, along with the criminals. [One of the criminals said] 'Jesus remember me when you come into your kingdom'"(Luke 23: 32-33, 42).

Jesus answered him, "Truly I tell you, today you will be with me in Paradise" (Luke 23: 43).

Here, the bible tells us that God can give even a criminal a last chance before death to turn to the Lord for salvation. Therefore, it's also reasonable to think that God might "seek out His lost sheep "right up until they draw their last breath [and] even if they are unconscious at the end." However, we have no way of knowing for sure what God will do. Thus, we can never take God for granted, but we must do as Isaiah 55:6 instructs: "Seek the Lord while he may be found; call on him while he is near."

What is the Lord like? We know from God's Word that He yearns to save men and women from the effects of sin. This is why he sent his Son, Jesus Christ, for our redemption. On the cross of Calvary, Christ took upon himself the sin of the world. He was made sin for us, and our guilt was imputed to him. There upon the cross, suffering the infinite penalty for our sins, our Savior said, 'It is finished' (John 19:30).

Therefore, the wages of sin have been paid forever by Christ. Those who place their trust in Him have His word that they will never perish. By dying on the cross, Christ has done everything appropriate and sufficient to make it unnecessary for anyone to find themself in eternal punishment.

# 11

# WHY DO SOME PROFESSED BELIEVERS FALL ASTRAY?

A lthough the issue of hypocrisy is sometimes raised by non-Christians as an excuse for rejecting Christianity, there are other times when the subject of those who stray from God is a real issue. Oftentimes, unbelievers have been truly disappointed and disillusioned by people who profess to be Christians but live ungodly lives, and this is a real barrier keeping the person from becoming a Christian. At least the non-church member admits he is not a Christian, so he isn't deceiving himself or anyone else.

Christians are supposed to be different, to be holy people. The church has set for itself high standards of love, of ethics, of service, of worship, of peace. Yet almost daily, newspaper headlines reveal examples of ministers, deacons, or church leaders who have been caught in unethical behavior such as adulterous relationships, financial exploitation, or some other inconsistency with what they profess to believe.

In addition, in their own communities non-Christians may observe church members, who seldom miss worship services and who claim to be concerned about the "spiritual dimension" of any problem, nevertheless, falling astray. They commit immoral actions such as extramarital affairs, financial dishonesty in business dealings, and other shameful conduct. Thus, unbelievers may sincerely ask, "Why are there so many hypocrites in the church?"

What is a hypocrite? A hypocrite is an actor, a person who pretends to know God, when he really does not. "The hypocrite is one engaged in intentional deception. He pretends to be more righteous than he actually is. The hypocrite is a moral playactor. He lives a lie. He claims to be free of faults which he practices covertly. His life is a guarded sham."[1]

Religious hypocrites make a charade of faith, go through the religious motions once a week. but the spiritual reality in their lives is nil. They are not true Christians at all, just hypocrites playing at religion. But even as there are lost people on the church rolls who are not real Christians, it must be stated that genuine Christians can sin and fail God.

Christians aren't perfect, nor do they claim to be. Those who have come to Christ in faith know they are not morally or spiritually superior. In fact, it is the awareness of their own shortcomings which motivates these folks in the first place to turn to Christ for forgiveness and help. As Billy Graham points out, all Christians fall short of Christ's perfection: "Jesus is the only perfect Man who ever lived. The rest of us are at best but repentant sinners, try as we may to follow His magnificent example; and the church is but turning a blind eye toward itself when it claims infallibility or perfection for itself or any of its members."[2]

The church cannot claim perfection for its body. Christians are as liable to make mistakes, to commit sin, and to do unworthy deeds as anyone else. The only difference is Christians have admitted their failures to God and are allowing him to change their lives. Barry Wood writes:

> Being a Christian is not a claim to having 'arrived." We are not supersaints sitting in judgment on the rest of the world. We ought to put signs over the doors of our churches which read, *Welcome: Sinners Only*, because that's the only kind of people there are. The only real difference between a saved sinner and a lost sinner is that the saved sinner has Christ helping him overcome temptation. But what a difference Jesus makes![3]

It is important not to confuse hypocrisy with sin. In fact, a biblical Christian is a person who admits he is a sinner. A hypocrite is someone who outwardly pretends to be good. The distinction between the two is important.

Jesus Christ had very stern words for people who were hypocrites, especially the religious leaders of the day: "Woe to you, scribes and Pharisees, hypocrites! For you are like whitewashed tombs which on the outside appear beautiful, but inside they are full of dead men's bones and all uncleanness. Even so you too outwardly appear righteous to men, but inwardly you are full of hypocrisy and lawlessness" (Matt. 23:27-28). The scribes and Pharisees made an outward display of godliness but inwardly did not know God. Seeking the plaudits of men, they took pride in their knowledge of the law and the rituals, but their self-righteousness kept them from seeing their own sin.

Today, also, there are religious pretenders in the church who think they're fooling others. But God cannot be deceived and will one day tell these modern Pharisees the awful words: "I never knew you; depart from Me, you who practice lawlessness" (Matt. 7:23). Christ uttered harsh words against religious dissemblers because of the enormous damage that hypocrisy can cause. When religious fraud is exposed in the lives of church members, many people are hurt and disillusioned. One hypocrite can cause not only the loss of his own credibility but also the credibility of others in the church.

Hypocrisy is a very serious matter. But just because the church contains hypocrites does not mean that all Christians are hypocritical. Kenneth Boa and Larry Moody note:

> Hypocrisy, then, is a reality that has not been rooted out of the Christian church. But it would be wrong to condemn all Christians as hypocrites just as it would be wrong to condemn the medical profession because of wrong diagnoses and ineffective treatments, as well as certain instances of malpractice. For every example of hypocrisy in the church, counter-examples of genuinely transformed lives can be multiplied.[4]

Most church members are dedicated, genuine Christians. Non-Christians should not let the few hypocrites in the church keep them from knowing or worshiping God. No one ought to miss out on a relationship with Jesus Christ because of someone else's inconsistency and hypocrisy. Jesus offers his perfect righteousness to imperfect people who turn to him in repentence. How foolish it would be for anyone to let resentment against hypocritical behavior keep them from receiving this priceless gift.

Instead, scripture tells us to submit to the Lord with obedient hearts: "Come, let us bow down in worship, let us kneel before the Lord our Maker; for he is our God"(Psalm 95:6-7). And warns us: "See to it . . . that none of you has a sinful, unbelieving heart that turns away from the living God" (Hebrews 3:12). It also instructs us: "You will seek me and find me when you seek me with all your heart" (Jeremiah 29:13).

# NOTES

## CHAPTER ONE

[1]1 Peter 3:15 (*NIV Study Bible, Large Print*).

[2]N. E. Kurz, *A Personal Grief: Finding Faith Through Loss* (Bolivar, MO: Dogwood Publishing, 2025), pp.21-23

[3]Deborah Cusick, *Beyond the Ends of the Earth: A Quest for Life's Purposes* (Tampa, FL: Gatekeeper Press, 2025), p. 159.

[4]*Ibid*, p. 2.

[5]John Warwick Montgomery, *Faith Founded on Fact* (Nashville, TN: Thomas Nelson, 1978), pp. 39-40.

[6]*Ibid*, p. 40.

[7]Paul Little, *Know Why You Believe* (Wheaton, IL: Victor Books, 1983), p. 147.

[8]Psalm 86:9-10 (*NIV Study Bible, Large Print*).

[9]Psalm 95:3-5 (*NIV Study Bible, Large Print*).

[10]Https://www.newsweek.com/hindu-festival-india-world-largest-religious-gatering-maha-kumbh-2013884, p. 2.

[11]*Ibid.*, p. 4.

[12]https://www.patheos.com/blogs/lotuspond/2025/01/maha-kumbh-mela-prayagraj-2025/, p.2.

[13]*Ibid.*, p. 9.

[14]*Ibid.*, p. 7.

[15]Hosea 4:6 (*NIV Study Bible, Large Print*).

[16]Hosea 4:1-3 (*NIV Study Bible, Large Print*).

[17]Hosea 4:19 (*NIV Study Bible, Large Print*).

[18]Hosea 13:3 (*NIV Study Bible, Large Print*).

[19]Psalm 1:4 (*NIV Study Bible, Large Print*).

[20]Jeremiah 18:6-10 (*NIV Study Bible, Large Print*).

[21]2 Kings 23:30 (*NIV Study Bible, Large Print*).

[22]2 Kings 24:20 (*NIV Study Bible, Large Print*).

[23]J. Andrew Dearman, *The NIV Application Commentary: Jeremiah & Lamentations* (Grand Rapids, MI, Zondervan, 2002), P. 190.

[24]https://foxnews.com/lifestyle/inside-donald-trumps-relationship-god-his-own-words, pp. 1-2.

[25]*Ibid.*, p. 2.

[26]*Ibid.*, pp. 3-4.

[27]*Ibid.*, p. 5.

<sup>28</sup>*Ibid.*, p. 5.

<sup>29</sup>*Ibid.*, p. 6.

<sup>30</sup>*Ibid.*, p. 3.

<sup>31</sup>*Ibid.*, p. 2.

<sup>32</sup>*Ibid.*, p. 1-7.

<sup>33</sup>Daniel 2:21 (*NIV Study Bible, Large Print*).

<sup>34</sup>Compiled by John R. Rice, Joy Rice Martin, *Soul Stirring Songs & Hymns* (Murfreesboro, TN: Sword of the Lord Publishers, 1972), p. 405.

<sup>35</sup>Isaiah 1:7 (*NIV Study Bible, Large Print*).

<sup>36</sup>Psalm 46:1-2, 7 (*NIV Study Bible, Large Print*).

<sup>37</sup>2 Corinthians 4:4 (*NIV Study Bible, Large Print*).

<sup>38</sup>Ephesians 6:11-12 (*NIV Study Bible, Large Print*).

<sup>39</sup>Proverbs 28:4-5 (*KJV Study Bible*).

<sup>40</sup>Proverbs 29:2 (*KJV Study Bible*).

## CHAPTER TWO

<sup>1</sup>Lloyd Ogilve, *Ask HimAnything*(Dallas,TX: WORD Incorporated, 1981), p. 9.

[2]Alan Richardson, *Christian Apologetics*(New York, NY: Harper and Row, 1947), p. 22. Reprinted by permission of SCM Press, London, England.

[3]Pierson, *"The Heresy of Simple Faith,"* p. 342.

[4]Edward John Carnell, *Christian Commitment* (New York, NY: Macmillan, 1957), p. 142.

[5]Ibid., pp. 82-83.

[6]Jay Kesler, *Breakthrough* (Wheaton, IL: Campus Life Books, 1981), p. 24.

[7]J. B. Phillips, *Your God is Too Small* (New York, NY: Macmillan, 1961), p. 8. Additional rights granted by Epworth Press, Cambridge, England.

[8]Colin Chapman, *The Case for Christianity* (Grand Rapids, MI: Eerdmans, 1981), p. 123.

[9]C.S.Lcwis, *The Weight of Glory and Other Addresses* (New York, NY: Macmillan, 1980), p. 28. Reprinted by permission of HarperCollins, London, England.

[10]Josh McDowell, *Answers to Tough Questions* (San Bernardino, CA: Here's Life, 1983), p. 119.

[11]Terry Miethe, *A Christian's Guide to Faith and Reason* (Minneapolis, MN: Bethany House, 1987), p. 29.

[12]Carncll, *Christian Commitment*, p. 198.

# CHAPTER THREE

[1]Lewis Carroll, *Alice's Adventure in Wonderland and Through the Looking Glass* (New York, NY: Parents Magazine Press, 1964), pp. 71-72.

[2]McDowell, *Answers to Tough Questions*, pp. 149-150.

[3]C. E. M. Joad, "The Plight of the Intellectual," *The Fate of Man* (New York, NY: George Braziller, 1961), p. 367.

[4]M. Vernon Davis, "Christianity Needs Performance, Not Defense," *Word and Way*, 12 November 1987, p. 11.

[5]Miethe, *A Christian's Guide to Faith and Reason*, p. 114.

[6]Calvin Miller, *A Hunger for Meaning* (Downers Grove, IL: Inter-Varsity Press, 1984), p. 12.

[7]Taken from the book, THE INTELLECT AND BEYOND by Oliver Barclay, Copyright©l985 by the .2ondervan Corporation. Used by permission.

[8]Francis Schaeffer, *The Complete Works of Francis A. Schaeffer*, Volume I (Westchester, IL: Crossway Books, 1982), p. 154.

[9]Miethe, *A Christian'sGuide to Faith and Reason*, pp. 17-18.

[10]F. R. Beattie, *Apologetics* (Richmond, VA: Presbyterian Committee of Publication, 1903), pp. 37-38.

[11]Miethe, *A Christian's Guide to Faith and Reason*, p. 120.

[12]Excerpt from *Faith and Reason* by Nels F.S. Ferre. Copyright 1946 by Harper and Brothers Publishers, Inc., copyright renewed, 1974 by Mrs. Nels F.S. Ferre. Reprinted by permission of HarperCollins Publishers.

[13]Little, *Know Why You Believe*, p. 142.

[14]Richard Dugan, *How to Know You'll Live Forever* (Minneapolis, MN: Bethany House, 1984), p. 133.

[15]Carnell, *Christian Cmnmitment*, pp. 76-77.

## CHAPTER FOUR

[1]Kenneth Boa and Larry Moody, *I'm Glad You Asked* (Wheaton, IL: Victor Books, 1982), p. 64.

[2]LewisDrummond and Paul Baxter, *How to Respond to a Skeptic* (Chicago, IL: Moody Press, 1986), p. 23.

[3]Pinnock. *Reason Enough*, p. 34.

[4] *Ibid.*

[5]Ibid., p. 35.

[6]Swindoll, *Growing Deep in the Christian Life*, pp. 54-55.

[7]Little, *Know Why You Believe*, pp. 148-149.

[8]Harry Blamines, *On Christian Truth* (Ann Arbor, MI: Servant Publications, 1983), pp. 7-8.

[9]Ferre, *Faith and Reason*, p. 193.

[10]From the book *Questions Non-Christians Ask* by Barry Wood, Copyright©1977 by Fleming H. Revell. Used by permission of Fleming H. Revell Company.

## CHAPTER FIVE

[1]Little, *Know Why You Believe*, p. 139.

[2]Cliffe Knechtle, *Give Me an Answer* (Downers Grove, IL: Inter-Varsity Press, 1986), p. 19.

[3]C.S. Lewis, *Mere Christianity* (New York, NY: Macmillan, 1952), p. 43. Reprinted by permission of HarperCollins, London, England.

[4]See books like: George Eldon Ladd, *I Believe in the Resurrection of Jesus* (Eerdmans, 1975); Michael Green, *The Empty Cross of Jesus* (Inter-Varsity Press, 1984); John Wenham, *Easter Enigma: Are the Resurrection Accounts in Conflict?* (Zondervan, 1984); Frank Morrison, *Who Moved the Stone* (Zondervan, 1958); and Terry Miethe (ed.), Gary Habermas, and Antony G. N. Flew, *Did Jesus Rise From the Dead? The Resurrection Debate* (Harper and Row, 1989) has an excellent bibliography.

[5]McDowell, *Answers to Tough Questions*, p. 64.

[6]Taken from the book, REASON TO BELIEVE by RC. Sproul, Copyright©1981 by RC. Sproul. Used by permission of Zondervan Publishing House.

[7]Little, *Know Why You Believe*, p. 131.

## CHAPTER SIX

[1]There is a growing body of literature from both sides regarding this "conflict." The following books are valuable: Donald Mackay, *Science and the Quest for Meaning* (Eerdmans, 1982); Charles Hummel, *The Galileo Connection: Resolving Conflicts between Science and the Bible* (Inter-Varsity, 1986); Rohen Gange, *Origins and Destiny: A Scientist Examines God's Handiwork* {Word Books, 1986); A. E. Wilder Smith, *Man's Origin, Man's Destiny* (Bethany House Publishers, 1968); Norman Macbeth, *Darwin Retried: An Appeal to Reason* (Gambit, 1971); Charles Thaxton, Walter Bradley, and Roger Olsen, *The Mystery of Life's Origin: Reassessing Current Theories* (Philosophical Library, 1984); and Henry Morris and Gary Parker, *What is Creation Science?* (Creation-Life Publishers, Inc., 1982).

[2]But not all Christian Scholars hold to a "young earth" theory; see Davis Young, *Christianity and the Age of the Earth* (Eerdmans, 1982).

[3]Don Stewart, *99 Questions People Ask Most About the Bible* {Wheaton, IL: Tyndale House, 1982), p. 107.

[4]*Ibid.*, p. 100.

[5]For the best statement of just what biblical inerrancy does entail see "The Chicago Statement on Biblical Inerrancy," pp. 493-502 in *Inerrancy*, edited by Norman L. Geisler (Zondervan, 1979).

[6]Reprinted by permission by Macmillan Publishing Company from *Is God a Creationist?* edited by Roland Mushat Frye. Copyright© 1983 by Charles Scribner's Sons.

[7]Davis Young, "Christianity and the Age of the Earth," in *Is God a Creationist?*, p. 84.

[8]Edwin Olson, "Hidden Agenda Behind the Evolution/Creationist Debate," in *Is God a Creationist?*, p. 40.

[9]Young, "Christianity and the Age of the Earth," pp. 92-93.

[10]*Ibid.*, p. 86.

[11]Langdon Gilkey, "Creationism: The Roots of the Conflict," in *Is God A Crtationist?*, p. 64.

[12]Dean, *How Can We Believe?*, p. 20. Permission granted by the author, who holds the copyright.

[13]Michael Green, *Faith for the Non-Religious* {Wheaton, IL: Tyndale House, 1979), pp. 37-39.

[14]David Fidd and Peter Toon, *Real Questions* (Batavia, IL and Herts, England: Lion, 1984), p. 85.

[15]Wilbur Garrett, "Where Did We Come From?", *National Geographic*, October 1988, p. 434.

[16]John Putman, "The Search for Modern Humans," *National Geographic*, October 1988, p. 460.

[17]Jack Wood Sears, *Conflict and Harmony in Science and the Bible* (Grand Rapids, MI: Baker Book House, 1969), p. 13.

[18]Young, "Christianity and the Age of the Earth," p. 88.

## CHAPTER SEVEN

[1]McDowell, *Answers to Tough Questions*, p. 39.

[2]See: Jon Buell and 0. Quentin Hyder, *Jesus: God, Ghost, or Guru?* (Zondervan, 1978).

[3]Lewis, *Mere Christianity*, pp. 55-56.

[4]C. S. Lewis, *Miracles* (New York, NY: Macmillan, 1960), p. 109. Reprinted by permission of HarperCollins, London, England.

[5]From: *More Than a Carpenter.* By: Josh McDowell©1977. Used by permission of Tyndale House Publishers, Inc. All Rights Reserved.

[6]Philip Schaff, *The Person of Christ* {New York, NY: American Tract Society, 1913), pp. 94-95, 97.

[7]John R W. Stott, *Basic Christianity* (Grand Rapids, MI: Eerdrnans, 1983), p. 40.

[8]Lewis Sperry Chafer, *Systematic Theology* (Dallas, TX: Dallas Theological Seminary Press, 1947), p. 21.

[9]See: Miethe, Habermas, Flew, *Did Jesus Rise From the Dead? The Resurrection Debate* (Harper and Row, 1989).

[10]Michad Green, *Man Alive* (Downers Grove, IL: Inter-Varsity Press, 1968), p. 54.

## CHAPTER EIGHT

[1]See: Terry Miethe, *The New Christian's Guide to Following Jesus* (Minneapolis, MN: Bethany House, 1984). His excellent chapter on "The Problem of Evil" contains a full discussion of the Augustine solution.

[2]Excerpt from *Philosophy of Religion* by Elton Trueblood. Copyright©1957 by Elton Trueblood. Reprinted by permission of HarperCollins Publishers.

[3]C. S. Lewis, *The Problem of Pain* (New York, NY: Macmillan, 1962), p. 26. Reprinted by permission of Harper Collins, London, England.

[4]*Ibid.*, pp. 33-34.

[5]Dean, *How Can We Believe?*, pp. 37-38. Permission granted by the author, who holds the copyright.

[6]Pat Robertson, *Answers To 200 Of Life's Most Probing Questions* (Nashville, TN: Thomas Nelson Publishers, 1984), p. 20.

[7]Lewis, *The Problem of Pain*, p. 40.

[8]John Allan and Gus Eyre, *A Field Guide to Christianity* (Chicago, IL: Moody Press, 1986), p. 161. Reprinted by permission of Paternoster Press, Exeter, England.

[9]Drummond and Baxter, *How to Respond to a Skeptic*, p. 42.

[10]Lewis, *The Problem of Pain*, p. 93.

[11]Billy Graham, *Facing Death and the Lift After* (Dallas, TX: WORD Incorporated 1987), p. 90.

122 A REASONABLE FAITH

12Field and Toon, *Real Questions*, p. 89.

13Knechtle, *Give Me An Answer*, p. 56.

14Littlc, *Know Why You Believe*, pp. 127-128.

## CHAPTER NINE

1McDowell, *Answers to Tough Questions*, p. 2.

2Paul Little, *Know What You Believe* (Wheaton, IL: Victor Books, 1984), p. 10.

3Stewart, *99 Questions People Ask Most About the Bible*, p. 90.

4Taken from: *Answering the Tough Ones* by David Dewitt. Copyright 1980. Moody Bible Institute of Chicago. Moody Press. Used by permission.

5See: F. F. Bruce, *Are the New Testament Documents Reliable?* (Eerdmans, 1960); and John A T. Robinson, *Can We Trust the New Testament?* (Eerdmans, 1977).

6Montgomery, *History and Christianity*, p. 29.

7Fenton Hort and Brooke Westcott, *The New Testament in the Original Greek* (New York, NY: Macmillan, 1881),"Vol. 1, p. 561.

8Stewart, *99 Questions People Ask Most About the Bible*, p. 71.

9See: Gary Habermas, *The Verdict of History: Conclusive Evidence for the Life of Jesus* (Nashville, TN: Thomas Nelson, 1988).

[10]Wood, *Questions Non-Christians Ask*, p. 18.

[11]McDowell, *Answers to Tough Questions*, p. 75.

[12]Billy Graham, *Peace With God* (Dallas, TX: WORD BOOKS, 1984), pp. 24-25.

## CHAPTER TEN

[1]Harold Bryson, *The Reality of Hell and the Goodness of God* (Wheaton, IL: Tyndale House, 1984), pp. 86-87.

[2]"Evangelism not SBC Priority, Charges HMB's Banks," *Word and Way*, 11 August 1988, p. 12.

[3]William Spurrier, *Guide to the Christian Faith* (New York, NY: Charles Scribner's Sons, 1952), pp. 163-164.

[4]Pinnock, *Reason Enough*, p. 110.

[5]Dewitt, *Answering the Tough Ones*, pp. 65-66.

[6]Wood, *Questions Non-Christians Ask*, p. 100.

[7]Dewitt, *Answering the Tough Ones*, p. 67.

[8]https://www.thedivinemercy.org/articles/there-one-last-chance-be-saved, p. 2.

[9]*Ibid.*

## CHAPTER ELEVEN

[1]Sproul, *Reason to Believe*, p. 77.

[2]Graham, *Peace With God*, p. 181.

[3]Wood, *Questions Non-Christians Ask*, p. 51.

[4]Boa and Moody, *I'm Glad You Asked*, p. 166.